Ready, Mindset, Grow!

Nuggets Mined from the Leadership Journeys

James D. Johnson

Wisdom Editions

Minneapolis

Wisdom
Editions
Minneapolis

FIRST EDITION JUNE 2021
Ready, Mindset Grow! Nuggets Mined from the Leadership Journeys.
Copyright © 2021 by James D. Johnson
All rights reserved.

Printed in the United States of America.
10 9 8 7 6 5 4 3 2 1

ISBN: 978-1-950743-56-8

Cover and interior design: Gary Lindberg
Cover and interior illustrations: Paul Malchow

Ready, Mindset, Grow!

Nuggets Mined from the
Leadership Journeys

To Timothy Leahy and leaders like him who have the courage and vision to invest deeply in the people in their enterprises

Table of Contents

Foreword

Discover, measure and grow ... repeat ... repeat ... repeat! That's the journey that Jim Johnson has been on for many years as both a student of leadership and as a coach to leaders. Discovery is the first step of the process that is essential to growth. It is often a surprise to leaders that they really cannot see their own behavior; however, it is the rare individual that can. That makes discovery essential in the process of uncovering how others see you as a leader. Jim has been a master of using tools and interviews to paint the picture for each leader of how others see them and measuring the gap between that perspective and how they see themselves. In the measurement of that gap lies the growth opportunity for each of us as leaders, whether that is in our organizations, families or communities. Jim has guided this process so many times with heartfelt caring and sensitivity that the insights in this book are pearls, which should be considered by everyone wanting to grow and improve. Finally, it is a never-ending process that will be repeated over and over again as you discover new aspects of your leadership style, measure your gaps and grow to fill them.... It is indeed a life-long journey full of enjoyment and fulfillment.

C. Joseph "Joe" Atteridge
Managing Partner
The Pacific Institute

Introduction

What a long, strange trip it's been.

—Grateful Dead

3M is a brand that I have long admired. The company we see today was, as Tom Peters said in his book, *In Search of Excellence,* founded on failure. Their leaders had the resilience and efficacy to face their crisis head-on, be vulnerable enough to acknowledge and own their situation, envision a future opportunity, pivot, empower their people, and execute to become the innovative giant we know today. I'd like to think (who wouldn't?) that I have displayed some of those qualities in my career. Failing forward is an art form and a testament to resilience and innovation.

People often ask me how I became an executive coach. The answer is, it's complicated.

My path was not the straight line that many in the consulting world experience. Although I earned a degree in Social and Behavioral Sciences at Johns Hopkins University, I had more of a passion for the game of Lacrosse that I nourished there than for my professional training. My first jobs were as a teacher and coach in high schools in the States and in Europe.

My first crisis, the accidental death of my father in 1977 when I was twenty-six, brought me back to my folks' home in Colorado to look after my infirm mom and high school-aged sister. After squaring away the estate, I moved up into the mountains and worked my way from line worker in a ski resort to running its resort association. From there, a series of career moves led me to progressively senior marketing roles in the tourism, hotel and gaming industry in Nevada. That is where I came face to face with my second crisis in 1990: I was given the opportunity to "re-examine my career options." There I was, with an eighteen-month-old and a second on the way, operating on the high wire without a net.

My wife and I examined the options in front of us, and we agreed that I should go toward creating a consulting business based on strategic planning work for small and mid-sized businesses. I found that it was relatively easy to get business leaders to sign up for the planning portion. Who doesn't love designing ways to slay the dragon? The challenge was to get the leader I was sitting across from to do what was required to implement the necessary changes for the enterprise.

Many of the leaders I worked with early on had a fairly fixed mindset—their inability to see options limited them when the dragon showed up at their door. It became evident that if my strategic planning work were to bear fruit and thus create referrals and repeat business, I needed to dive into the ways to help these leaders and their teams embrace change. One of the best senior leaders I ever worked for, Pat Cruzen, had introduced his leadership team, including me, to The Pacific Institute run by Lou and Diane Tice. They had created a system to educate people about the psychological underpinnings of change and achieving one's potential. It offered a tremendous toolset to help energize my practice.

I remember teaching high school kids about algebra and having to endure the inevitable question, "When am I ever going to use this in real life?" I should have said, "ask any computer programmer." It humbled me to remember that as I plunged back into my training after many years away from it as I worked to help leaders begin to appreciate the psychological side of leadership, sometimes inappropriately labeled "soft-skills."

That was still not enough. Prospective business leaders that I pitched had difficulty understanding how these soft skill pieces helped their business. I needed something that would quantify this side of their actions and help me connect it to traditional business measures.

Enter Michael J. O'Brien. In those days, he was heading up business development for Human Synergistics, a behavioral research company focused on determining the best combination of behaviors for individual and business interaction, commonly known as organizational culture. His insights provided me a way to connect where I had started my consulting journey to what I could do for the leaders and their enterprises.

It was a subtle and gradual change from strategic planning to change management to leadership coaching. Today, my consulting practice centers on helping leaders appreciate their role in shaping and influencing an organization's culture and the resulting business outcomes. I help them see the blind spots that they and their team have that hold them back from achieving superior performance for their people and themselves. As the leaders focus on this effort to connect everyone to the larger purpose of the enterprise, the outcomes they seek naturally materialize. It is very rewarding to witness their transformation and that of their organization.

It has been my privilege and good fortune to work with thousands of leaders like Brian Ness of the Idaho Transportation Department, Mike Leahy of Leahy-IFP and Tim Owings of Sierra Nevada Corporation and others who have been hungry to improve their ability to cause good things to happen within their organizations. I have observed and worked with them and have lately begun to write about what I have experienced. This book is intended to provide approaches to better ways to lead team members now and in the future.

In my experience, only those who truly want to improve seek the opportunity to grow and develop. It is my hope that this collection of stories and insights stimulates readers to find their path improved, satisfying and meaningful.

JJ

Prologue
Leadership Matters

*Leadership is unlocking people's
potential to become better.*

—*Bill Bradley*

Leadership. We know it when we see it, good and bad. We know that it matters ... history books are filled with examples of both and where it has led us. Fortunes have been made and lost because of it. Political movements and religious followings have thrived because of leadership.

Leadership is a prized commodity in every aspect of society. Nevertheless, good leadership is not universal. If you were to guess, what percentage of all business supervisors and managers in business today are viewed as strong leaders?

(A) 85%

(B) 67%

(C) 50%

(D) 30%

According to Conference Board research, the answer is (D). This means that fewer than 1-in-3 managers today pass muster. This deficit in leadership know-how profoundly restrains organizational performance—not to mention employee engagement, loyalty and productivity. Naturally, this dearth of skill in such pivotal positions ripples throughout the enterprise and reflects on the performance of the customer-facing members and those responsible for delivering the product to market. It is not the CEO who interacts with the consumer; more likely, it is someone

7

who is far less well-paid and trained. The leadership and stakeholders are taking the risk that those workers will uphold the promise in the organization's brand.

As we will discuss, *if you do what you did, you'll get what you got.* There is a clear reason employee engagement scores across the world have not meaningfully improved in over two decades. The way we have collectively led and managed does not suit the needs of twenty-first-century workers. By getting the culture right, leaders can successfully realize a healthy return on investment for their brand.

JJ's Takeaways

- We know it when we see it, we know that it is important – Leadership makes a material difference.

- For those who want to make a difference, developing leadership provides concrete traction now.

Part I
What We Need from Leaders

If your actions inspire others to dream more, learn more, do more and become more, you are a leader.

—John Quincy Adams

The Art of Appreciative Inquiry proceeds from a different way of looking at our actions and using the lessons to improve. There was a time when coaches and teachers would spend inordinate amounts of time going over what went wrong, literally replaying the error repeatedly in an effort to erase the flaws. Ironically, since we are teleological beings and we go toward what we are thinking about, this method only served to reaffirm the flaws, causing their repetition.

Appreciative Inquiry starts with the analysis of What Went Well? That analysis is followed by What Must We Do Better? No Pollyanna world here. It requires being fully grounded in what actually occurred, but instead of a focus on what went wrong, which naturally produces pushback and justifications, the emphasis is on growth and learning to be able to do something different the next time and see improved results.

Studying what leaders did and discovering what they learned and how they grew and improved is an effective way of acquiring leadership skills. The stories we witness give us great insight into how leaders can better serve their people.

Good Leaders Cannot Get Too Far Out in Front of Their People

A great person attracts great people and knows how to hold them together.

—Johann Wolfgang Von Goethe

Can you imagine what the world would look like today had Winston Churchill failed to become Prime Minister during World War II? It almost happened because of his role in the spectacularly unsuccessful Dardanelles Campaign two decades earlier in World War I. In that affair, over 142,000 British, Dominion and French troops were killed or wounded. Although it would be hard to see a silver lining from this disaster, there was one. Fortunately for all of us, Churchill learned from the experience and, although he made other mistakes in his career, this discovery stayed with him and informed his future leadership.

Few people have engaged in as much wartime leadership as Winston Churchill. He played active roles as a soldier and correspondent in the Boer War (1899–1902), First Lord of the Admiralty and a line officer in the British Army in World War I (1914–1917), and as First Lord of the Admiralty, Defense Minister and Prime Minister in World War II (1939–1945). He was widely credited with saving the Western World from Nazi domination because of his heroic leadership stand when England stood alone against the Germans in 1940.

His road to that display of courage and determination was bumpy and fraught with potholes, stumbles and miscalculations that branded him among many as a reckless, unreliable warmonger and sidetracked his political ambitions for many years. We are fortunate that he arrived at his appointment with destiny at all.

Gallipoli: How NOT to Wage War

One of his more famous setbacks occurred during World War I when, as First Lord of the Admiralty, he proposed attacking the Ottoman Empire with a strike at its heart: Constantinople (Istanbul). He believed that he could roll up the entire empire and capture the city by forcing the Dardanelles, a strait that traditionally demarks the boundary between Europe and the Middle East, and landing troops in an area called Gallipoli.

His strategy was based on the sobering reality that in western Europe, the war had ground to a slaughterhouse stalemate; an entire generation of European, Ottoman, British and Commonwealth young men gave their lives in a futile attempt to break through each other's lines. Churchill reasoned that a successful attack in this region would change the dynamics in the war and put enormous pressure on the Germans and their allies.

The plan of attack required close coordination between the British Army and its vaunted Navy, a tenuous thing at the best of times. Coordination was poor; sadly, the Navy did not live up to its reputation, and the Army was sluggish and executed poorly. The result was that the campaign failed badly. In addition to the lost lives, it also cost Churchill his post in the British Government.

Some have argued that his strategy would have worked had the Army and Navy worked better together, acting more decisively. However, in war, operational plans break down from all manner of unexpected problems and challenges. It is possible that even with these enhancements, the plan might still have failed. Conversely, it is more likely that, had the senior leadership team acted and communicated more effectively together, the Gallipoli incursion and subsequent disaster might not have occurred at all.

Public outrage at the horrific outcome demanded that the British War Cabinet conduct an inquiry into the attack. As a result of this after-action review, an important leadership issue emerged. Andrew Roberts in *Churchill: Walking with Destiny* writes, In the ensuing Interim Report of the Dardanelles Commission, published 12 February 1917, the following was noted:

Mr. Churchill thought that he was correctly

representing the collective views of the
Admiralty experts. But without in any way
wishing to impugn his good faith, it seems
clear that he was carried away by his sanguine
temperament and his firm belief in the success
of the undertaking which he advocated…
Mr. Churchill had obtained their support to
a less extent than he himself imagined…
Other members of the Council, and more
especially the Chairman [Prime Minister
Asquith], should have encouraged the
experts to give their opinion, and, indeed,
should have insisted upon their doing so.

Roberts, commenting on this in the book, added,
"A collective groupthink permeated the meeting of (the
Commission) of 13 January, encouraging optimism and
discouraging incisive questioning, a problem made all the
worse by [Admirals] Fisher's and Jackson's silence."

Leadership Lessons Learned from a Disaster

How many times have we seen people clam up or "get rolled"
in strategy discussions, especially with senior leaders present?
Many of those leaders got where they were by being able to
execute well. Often, they have great ideas and/or see more
clearly a solution to a pressing issue. Typically, they press
that advantage in strategy discussions with great conviction.
Often, team members "reluctantly go along." Is this one of
the reasons that two-thirds of all change initiatives fail to
achieve their stated goal or fail altogether?

There are two critical components in group decisions,
1) the Quality of the Solution; and 2) the Acceptance of
the Solution. While vision is important, a leader must

communicate that vision in a vivid and compelling manner so that those entrusted with executing the mission believe in it, wholly support the effort and enthusiastically follow through. Then, those leaders must relay the vision in a similar fashion so that all involved have confidence in the execution and can withstand the snags and setbacks that inevitably occur. A hallmark of great cultures is that information moves up and down throughout the organization with minimum distortion and maximum credibility.

On the other hand, those responsible to the leader for execution have a parallel obligation to ask the difficult questions necessary so they can wholeheartedly endorse and believe in the mission. In their book, *Extreme Ownership,* Leif Babin and Jocko Willink talk about the need for those responding to the leader to fully accept and endorse the vision s/he puts forth. If they are not able to believe in the vision or proposed strategy, they will not enthusiastically support its execution; consequently, the initiative will stumble or fail to produce the expected results. If they are unable to get satisfactory answers, they must press the leader to completely understand their concerns so the vision or strategy may be refined, revised or scrapped entirely. This requires a level of trust and courage among the leadership and team members to work properly. This can only happen in an organization whose culture fosters this kind of communication and is evidenced by the leaders having the level of humility to listen carefully and act appropriately.

In his role as First Sea Lord, Churchill's towering personality and overwhelming self-confidence created a blind spot in him to the dangers of the coordinated Army-Navy attack plan. At the same time, his key subordinates, Admirals Fisher and Jackson, failed to impress on Churchill their reluctance to pursue his plans. Their collective failure to achieve clarity cost hundreds of thousands of lives, set back the war effort, and substantially damaged Churchill's reputation and risked impacting the course of history.

Churchill benefited from a Growth Mindset. He learned valuable lessons from his actions in the Great War and employed them to considerable effect in World War II. He engaged his War Cabinet and the Allies much more effectively, collaboratively. And the rest, as they say ... fortunately for all of us, the results were markedly different.

Leaders succeed in creating engagement when they are crystal clear about their vision and the strategies they intend to employ. In addition, they need to be humble enough to recognize that those who implement that vision often have a stronger grasp on the day-to-day realities of execution. That means that leaders must seek input and listen attentively and carefully before proceeding. Team members who work closely with the leader must have the trust, courage and persistence to ensure that they obtain sufficient clarity and fully understand her approach so that they can endorse and enthusiastically support its execution. Otherwise, they must present clear and compelling information why an alternative approach is the better course. Anything left in the middle will likely result in a muddle, rendering less than satisfactory outcomes.

If You Do What You Did, You Will Get What You Got

Can you remember a time when you saw a group or a team whose talent and skills were clearly evident, but somehow, the results didn't pan out? How many times have we looked at an organization and said, "With that crew, they should be unstoppable?" Imagine our disappointment when all that talent doesn't deliver. The stock market has seen hundreds of these stories and their disappointed investors are legion.

How many times has poor leadership held us back? Teams and the individuals within often have substantially more potential than their current performance demonstrates. The skill of good leaders lies in creating the proper mindset, empowering the members to alter their habits, attitudes, beliefs and expectations. Operating through a growth mindset, they foster an environment where the members can perform at a higher level, closer to their full potential. In their book, *Extreme Ownership*, former Navy Seals Leif Babin and Jocko Willink demonstrated this concept in a vividly concrete fashion.

They described the grueling training regimen all candidates underwent in order to qualify for their elite unit. As a part of every day's training, crews were required to paddle out in inflatable rafts and race in the ocean surf outside San Diego. Day after day, one of the six competing crews consistently came in first. Another was frequently last. After a couple of weeks, the trainers swapped out boat commanders between the leading and trailing boats. When they did, an interesting thing happened: the crew that had originally finished last started winning while the other team continued to perform well because of the habits instilled by their original commander.

Have you ever been in a situation where someone in charge got everyone wound up and then headed in the wrong direction? There are many examples where we can see how poor leadership resulted in disappointing, sometimes tragic, results. Much of World War I highlighted the excruciating myopia displayed by commanders on both sides.

There were three enormous battles during that conflict fought near Passchendaele, Belgium. They were immortalized by Canadian physician Lieutenant-Colonel John McCrae in his poem "In Flanders Fields." The final conflict there, the Third Battle of Ypres, began on July 31, 1917. After three months of unrelenting, brutal fighting failed to break the stalemate, the English commander, General Douglas Haig, recklessly threw an additional four Canadian divisions into the charnel house.

Winston Churchill had opposed the General Staff's bankrupt strategy long before as a Cabinet member. Instead, he backed an expedition in the Bosporus to break the stalemate and create pressure in other theaters of the war. Sadly, it was a miserable tactical failure, costing him his post. Worse, 250,000 soldiers became casualties in this ill-executed mission.

As a consequence, he resigned in 1916 from the Admiralty on a point of principle and sought reinstatement to his commission as an officer and rejoined the army. He was sent to the front line, an extraordinary and unexpected measure of leadership. When the battle at Ypres unfolded, he was aghast at the slaughter.

He later wrote in his opus *The World Crisis*, "It cannot be said that "the Soldiers" [British General Staff] … did not have their way. They tried their sombre experiment to its conclusion. They took all they required from Britain. They wore down alike the manhood and the guns of the British Army almost to destruction. They did it in the face of the plainest warnings, and of arguments which they could not answer."

Every Remembrance Day (Veterans Day) residents of Canada, New Zealand, Australia and the UK wear poppies as boutonnieres to commemorate the fallen of these battles. How many thousands of soldiers on all sides were wounded or killed because of leaders with blinders to alternate solutions?

Churchill exemplified a different type of leader. Opinionated, bellicose and difficult to deal with, he was nevertheless nimble, creative and available to persuasion by those with more compelling arguments. During his first stint at the British Admiralty, he shook up a tradition-bound command staff. He was responsible for transforming the fleet from a coal-fired navy to a petroleum base and other innovations.

In a speech at the University of Berne in 1970, Lord Mountbatten observed that Churchill designed and commissioned a "land warship," what we now know as the tank. As the Minister of Munitions, he initiated the requirement that information routed upward be delivered "on one sheet of paper." He was renowned for his memos that required "Action This Day."

Undeterred by his setback at Gallipoli, he lobbied for and was posted back into the military and transferred to the Front. Returning to a familiar role as an Army officer, and despite the justifiable bias against politicians who secured military postings as a means of promoting their careers, Churchill quickly earned the support and respect of the men who served with him in Belgium.

Ultimately recalled from service on the Continent by the Prime Minister, Churchill was named Minister of Munitions, a post outside the Cabinet. Although pivotal for the war effort throughout, this ministry, sadly, underperformed. After he took over, he reorganized the entire operation, generating immediate and substantial increases in the production of tanks, machine guns, aircraft and mustard gas. As the champion of the development of the tank, derisively labeled "Winston's Folly," he persevered in its production. In a sound confirmation of his strategy, in November 1917, 378 British tanks helped capture 10,000 German prisoners. Roberts observed in his book *Churchill: Walking with Destiny*, that production through the Ministry had increased so much so that General Haig acknowledged that "Only in 1918 was it possible to conduct artillery operations independent of any limiting consideration other than that of transport."

Churchill was destined to face his greatest leadership challenge two decades later when Europe faced domination by the Fascist onslaught. Two previous Prime Ministers, Stanley Baldwin and Neville Chamberlain, had, with the best of intentions, driven England and the British Empire to the brink of servitude to Nazi Germany. In the face of overwhelming odds, Churchill steadied and then rallied his people as they withstood the juggernaut alone until the United States and the Soviet Union were dragged into the conflict.

Same people, different leaders, better outcomes. Winston Churchill, his mettle having been tested and wizened by past missteps during World War I, proved that there are no bad teams, only bad leaders.

JJ's Takeaways

- Leader/Subordinate and Team relations must rely on trust.

- Teams have unlimited potential – good leaders find the means to elicit excellence.

- Leaders must be humble enough to listen, learn and adjust.

- Implementers must adhere to their mission, courageously insisting on clarity to remain committed.

A Keewaydin "Halfway"—
Servant Leadership in Action

Service is the rent that you pay for room on this earth.

—*Shirley Chisholm*

The summer of my seventh grade, my parents thought it would be great if I spent the summer at a canoe camp in Ontario. They packed me up and sent me on an overnight train from my home in Colorado to Chicago, followed by another overnight train to Toronto and a day train up north to Lake Temagami. A one-hour ferry ride handled the last leg to Devil Island and Keewaydin Camp.

A Bracing Dip

The following day, we were all administered a swim test, which set the tone for my two-month stay in the Canadian woods. It consisted of jumping off the dock and proving we could swim a reasonable distance. I proudly jumped in to display my ability. As this was the last day of June, and Lake Temagami is 450 km (280 mi) due north of Toronto, the water was so cold that I almost jumped back up onto the dock out of sheer reflex! I could hardly draw a breath—some fun!

Canoeing was no joyride either. Paddling around in a lake was okay but going from one lake to another required gathering all the gear from the canoe and "portaging" across the ground to the next body of water.

We traveled in a group; in each canoe, we carried our foodstuffs and canvas tent, contained in and on a lidded box called a "wanigan" and our bedroll and clothes were stuffed into duffel bags, two to a canoe. The bedrolls were lashed together with a long leather strap called a "tump" line, made of a long length of leather with a wide, reinforced strip in the center. The wanigans and canoes were similarly outfitted with these tump lines. The boys would lift them onto their backs, and the strap would fit across the head so that the neck, back and shoulders bore the weight evenly. The three items, wanigan, bedrolls and canoe, were then carried one at a time across the portage to the new lake. The canoe was carried the entire distance by the stern man, and he would then walk back to the halfway point where the bow man had carried either the wanigan or the bedroll halfway, then returned to the portage's start to get the other item and carry it across. All sorts of fun!

The "Keewaydin Halfway"

Despite my lack of enthusiasm for the attraction of intermittent rain, wet clothes and mosquitos attacking at the most inconvenient personal moments, canoe camping imparted some valuable life lessons. One of them was the importance of a "Keewaydin Halfway." The bow man would carry the first load as much as two-thirds of the way to the other side because the stern man had the canoe, a much heavier load. He would then return and get the bedrolls and complete the portage to the other side. The stern man would then collect the wanigan at the halfway point and make his way to the spot to "put in," and the canoe parade would begin again—two months of portages and "Keewaydin Halfways."

All these years later, that value, impressed on me as a boy, has stayed with me in my work with executives. As servant leaders, what are we doing for those who are doing the "heavy lifting"?

According to Gallup's 2017 report, *State of the American Workplace*, [Only] "Three in 10 U.S. employees strongly agree[d] that, [with]in seven days, someone noticed and complimented them on their work. By moving that ratio to six in 10 employees, organizations could realize a 24% improvement in quality, a 27% reduction in absenteeism and a 10% reduction in shrinkage." These employees reported that they placed importance on the specificity and immediacy of providing recognition and that the most meaningful recognition came from their manager, followed by recognition from a leader or CEO, their manager's manager, customers and peers.

Go the Distance

As leaders, are we acting as the bow man and doing a "Keewaydin Halfway" for our people? Are we going that extra mile to ensure that they have clarity of mission and vision? Do they know why we are asking for their efforts? Do they have the right tools and environment to thrive? Do we help them understand why their job matters and is important? These simple, straightforward investments in our people and our internal value proposition yield enormous dividends on our external value proposition, our brand – and it isn't even necessary to wear insect repellant!

JJ's Takeaways

- Employee engagement is crucial to high performance.

- A mindset of Servant Leadership is a key factor in fostering engagement.

- Workers are acutely aware of leadership's actions on their behalf.

PART II
It's the Brand that Matters /
Culture is Everything

In business today, nothing happens
unless somebody makes a sale.

—*G. Thomas Dutmers*

Brand awareness is an absolute must in today's world. Organizations invest substantial resources in crafting a brand so that people will take the risk to purchase the good or service. That investment is carefully designed to shape the promise of what a buyer can expect.

On the other side of that same coin, the organizational culture determines what the buyer and the organization's members actually experience. As a result, the investment return on the brand's promise rests heavily on whether the leaders have effectively engaged those charged with delivering on that promise and empowered them to execute well.

Does Your Product Fulfill Your Promise?

The Case for Internal Branding Along with External Branding

You can't really think about your... customers...
unless you also think about your... people.

—*William Taylor*

How many companies do you know that say "our people are our most important asset"? Does that mean that they are at least as important as their customers? The question is, do these same companies spend as much time and energy on their "Internal Value Proposition" as they do with their "External Value Proposition"?

Marketing & HR—Boon or Bane?

If we were to examine a typical profit and loss statement, we would find, among other items, these two areas under general and administrative expenses: marketing (or something similar) and human resources (or something similar). Both can be viewed in one of two ways:

- A revenue generator
- A drag on profitability

In fact, it isn't always one or the other. Often, they are both, and they do not necessarily function independently of each other.

If we look at line items in Marketing, they are typically advertising, public relations, direct mail, social media and the like. When we boil down all of these functions, it's about resources for making a promise to prospective consumers about the product.

When we look at Human Resources, there are many functions such as onboarding, payroll, benefits and talent acquisition. Reduced to their essence, it is about resources for making (and keeping) promises to those whom the enterprise employs.

People are Always Responsible for the Product

Before I worked with organizations in my present role, I oversaw marketing within enterprises. The word on me was that I could outspend an unlimited budget. Doing what? Making promises—getting people to take a chance with their hard-earned money on our product. Although a lot of my experience in those days was in service-based products, the notion of generating trial is similar in product-based enterprises as well.

An industry that demonstrates my point is tourism and travel. Ski resorts are an excellent example. If you are a prospective customer, what are the promises you often see online, in commercials and magazines? Magnificent photos of spectacular vistas, snow-covered mountains, smiles and sunglasses. What an appeal!

In reality, when it comes to fulfilling that promise, for many, the last mile to the ski resort occurs in a car. When the customer finally arrives at the resort, often early in the morning, who is the first ski resort employee the customer is likely to encounter? The parking lot attendant, naturally. That employee, typically among the least well-paid, under-informed and possibly under-motivated, is completely in charge of creating the first step to an indelible customer experience. Is that first taste of the customer experience engaging or off-putting? Had management invested more in their internal value proposition, would the scales tip in favor of engaging?

Only One Chance to Make a Good First Impression

I'd be willing to wager that the marketing department, in crafting and deploying those incredibly attractive promises, easily outspent the labor cost and HR fringes for every one of those parking lot attendants. Gallup's most recent engagement survey found that roughly only one-third of American workers were "engaged." If two out of three customers responding to the terrific promise got an underwhelming first impression (or worse), what do you think the ROI would be on that fantastic promise? By contrast, best-in-class organizations get upwards of 70 percent engagement. So, was the HR expense a drag on profitability or a revenue enhancer? And why?

Marketers are some of the greatest storytellers in the world. They can target the right audience, craft the message to hit all the right notes and generate tremendous expectations and a willingness to try the product. If it is true that when something goes right, ten people hear about it, and when something goes awry, twenty-four people hear about it, then how long will it take for a good promise to make a "so-so" product look or feel even worse? What happens to the reputation of the enterprise when it is based on actual experience, not the "promise"? That gap between 35 percent and 70 percent engagement can have a substantial impact on revenues and profitability.

"Our People Make the Difference"

So, what is the fix? If an enterprise is going to invest in good storytelling, there must be an equal or greater effort to ensure that the product exceeds the promise. In the case of service businesses, it means that the least well-paid must be just as engaged and motivated as anyone else within the organization. Those companies selling "things" ignore the personal piece at their peril as well. After all, who fabricates and assembles those items, tests them, packages them, ships them and so on? Isn't it again often the least well-paid?

Organizations need to invest at least as much in their internal brand, their purpose, mission, vision, values and why they exist as they do in making appealing promises to their prospective customers. What is the culture of the organization? The "way we do things here"? What do we value? Do we clearly understand what is expected of us? Do we know where we are headed? The vividness and intensity of the pictures that leaders create in the minds of their employees is equally as important as the ones the marketers create for their customers.

So, to generate the enhanced ROI the marketers expect, take the time to invest deeply in the "most important asset" most organizations have, "their employees." In a later section, we will explore ways to cement the internal brand when we discuss Mission, Vision, Values and Engagement.

JJ's Takeaways

- Good marketing may generate trial – the product must match/exceed expectations.

- Product cannot match high expectations with disengaged workers.

- Companies must invest in leadership and employee development as much as/more than trial generation.

James Johnson

Part III
Higher Purpose

Think about it, there must be higher love
Down in the heart or hidden in the stars above
Without it, life is wasted time
Look inside your heart, I'll look inside mine

—*Steve Winwood, "Higher Love"*

Great organizations find effective ways of engaging their team members. They help their employees recognize that their efforts matter in accomplishing their goals. Their leaders know that most people seek to connect themselves to something greater than themselves. This helps them find meaning in their work and what they contribute to the enterprise.

The best-performing organizations seek to define and articulate an aspirational purpose suitable for their members so they can identify with and work toward that larger goal in a far more powerful way than just focusing on the commonly accepted outcomes used to measure performance in an enterprise. In so doing, it creates a more holistic connection with their jobs and inspires higher loyalty, attention to tasks at hand and the innovation necessary to thrive in today's intensely competitive marketplace. The conversation moves from what needs doing to why it matters to do it. It is a recipe for a far healthier workplace environment and likely leads to a better work/life balance.

Goalsetting: Connecting "My" Goals to "Our" Goals for Higher Engagement and Performance

When you ask people to go from where they are to someplace else, your task is to create a vision they can understand and will be willing to embrace.

—Roger Dean Duncan

What's in it for Me?

Rarely asked out loud, that "WIIFM" question frequently runs through the mind of anyone asked by a leader to perform a task. The standard answers often run somewhere in a range between "doing your job right allows you to stay here" and "when you do this well, you get to achieve one of your personal goals" (money, satisfaction, recognition, advancement, achievement). While these are acceptable motivators, in a competitive environment, "my goals" performances are simply table stakes. If these types of WIIFM goals are the only ones operating at this level, the employee may not even be engaged. In fact, according to Gallup's 2017 State of the American Workforce, barely one in three American workers is actively engaged. There are substantial performance gains to be obtained for those leaders who can exceed that figure.

Organizations that succeed in helping connect individual goals to organizational goals enjoy a substantial competitive advantage. It is as simple as the three laborers who were digging a series of trenches in a large field. When asked what they were there to do, the first replied, "Boss told me to dig a hole." The second answered, "My boss said we were putting up a BIG building." When the third laborer was asked, the answer was, "I've been told that we are digging the foundation for a great cathedral that is supposed to last for hundreds of years." I suspect that there is little surprise about which one dug the best trench.

An Organization's Purpose

The laborers achieved their WIIFM's as they individually viewed them. Certainly, each was paid for the time spent completing the task. The workers all received resources (pay) to pursue their personal goals made possible by the work they performed. However, the vivid clarity that the third laborer's leader provided about the end result of the project helped transform the effort of the employee from a "my" goal of a "paycheck" to an "our" goal of "purpose."

In an effort to increase productivity, enlightened organizations recognize that employee well-being and engagement matters. Unfortunately, many employers confuse satisfaction with being "happy." While free yoga at the office, catered lunches and gym reimbursements may be attractive and are possibly useful for some, over time, they become expected as a part of the package and no longer viewed as extras. Consequently, the kinds of rewards and perks offered are misaligned with what generates higher performance. Employees seek fulfillment in their jobs; they want to know that what they do at work matters. Just as we saw with the workers digging the foundation, people easily respond to doing their best work when they know they are fulfilling the purpose of the organization. In fact, according to Gallup, 60 percent of employees say the ability to do what they do best in a role is "very important" to them. Consequently, when engagement becomes an afterthought or gets confused with happiness, employees remain unfulfilled, pushing them in the wrong direction.

Connecting the Dots

Purpose provides an organization the opportunity to be clear in its mission. Clarity delivers solid performance advantages. In the Gallup study, six in ten US employees strongly agreed that they clearly knew what was expected of them. By moving that ratio to eight in ten employees, organizations could realize a 14 percent reduction in turnover, a 20 percent reduction in safety incidents and a 7 percent increase in productivity.

Clarity also provides employees with a foundation for performing their tasks well. Because doing their best work is something employees seek, companies providing that opportunity obtain better outcomes. For example, four in ten US employees currently strongly agree that at work, they have the opportunity to do what they do best every day. By moving that ratio to eight in ten employees, organizations could realize an 8 percent increase in customer engagement scores, a 14 percent increase in profitability and a 46 percent reduction in safety incidents.

Our Goals—Our Brand

Transforming WIIFM into "our" goals has other benefits. Connecting employees to mission affirms the importance of their work which naturally increases their engagement. In a later segment, Mission—Pointing a Way to True North, I discuss the power of a clear mission and its ability to generate engagement among team members. According to Gallup, organizations that succeed in increasing from an average of four in ten to eight in ten the connection of employees to the mission and the sense that their work is important stand to realize a 41 percent reduction in absenteeism, a 50 percent drop in patient safety incidents and a 33 percent improvement in quality. With this level of engagement, employers can feel confident that their brand is protected and that employees will deliver on their promise.

The other major benefit is that leaders can respond authentically to the WIIFM question and ensure that employees clearly understand their roles and that their contribution matters.

It is only natural when leaders ask their people to act that the WIIFM question be first in the employees' minds. When leaders succeed in linking "my goals" to "our goals," the enterprise gains tremendous leverage in the pursuit of its objectives and fulfilling its purpose. Improved traditional outcome measures naturally follow.

JJ's Takeaways

- It is natural for employees to analyze job assignments in terms of their self-interest.

- Leaders must help employees connect their personal goals to the higher purpose of the organization.

Connect to Purpose for
a Robust Culture

*Identify a purpose mammoth enough
and you can move a train without the engine.*

—Hermann J. Steinherr

In the heartwarming movie *Hidden Figures*, the overlooked and crucial contributions from a pivotal moment in American history are revealed. Through historical footage, we are treated to President John F. Kennedy speaking about NASA's mission to land a man on the moon. How giddy and exciting must it have been to hear him utter those words? In those days, the threat of nuclear holocaust was all too real. It was present in everyone's lives. The Space Race directly addressed the threat posed by the USSR, pitting US technology and resources against theirs in an existential struggle. To go to the moon was at once an expression of confidence in a potentially peaceful future, the capability of the team at NASA and the American spirit.

People were riveted to their television sets throughout the decade as the mission unfolded. President Kennedy galvanized an entire country behind a seemingly mind-boggling task: to send astronauts to the moon and return them safely to earth. The team at NASA easily understood and connected with the mission, vision and values that President Kennedy espoused. In the same way, leaders and organizations that succeed in connecting their people to a greater purpose can expect to reap the rewards of a robust culture along with healthy outcomes.

Leadership's Role in Purpose

A few years ago, Lou Tice, founder of The Pacific Institute, toured the manufacturing facility at the British medical manufacturing firm Smith and Nephew. He stopped to ask an older woman who was winding bandages on the shop floor what she did there every day. Her reply was simple and profound: "We relieve suffering."

Dr. Michael DeBakey was one of the greatest practitioners in the field of cardiovascular surgery. One day at Methodist Hospital in Houston, he was observed talking to one of the janitors before moving on to complete rounds. When the janitor was asked what they talked about, he replied that Dr. Debakey had asked him about his family and how he was doing his job at the hospital. When he was asked what he did there, he said proudly, "Dr. DeBakey and I, we save lives together."

What these people had in common was as much what they *didn't* say as what they did. When asked, neither of them described the tasks that they performed. Instead, their leaders had succeeded in helping them connect the job designed for them to perform to the larger outcome of the enterprise. Do you think that these two were engaged and had a "want to" approach to their jobs? What is the likelihood that their leadership communicated with them frequently about the purpose of what they were doing? When people can connect to the purpose leaders propose, they can see how what they do for the enterprise matters. When this happens, engagement soars and the constructive culture gets strong reinforcement.

Leadership Tools for Connecting to Purpose

How many organizations have mission statements that people recite easily? If people in an organization are unclear on what they are expected to accomplish, it's difficult to create a lot of energy to be impeccable in its execution. If a mission statement is too lengthy, leaders should develop a "bumper sticker" phrase that communicates what the organization does. Leadership should be prepared to revise mission or vision statements to hone this connection to purpose. One of my clients recently revised their vision statement because it became apparent that people were not making the connection between their work and the picture the organization had attempted to create. A subsequent effort to capture the "end state" involved everyone at the company; the result was an aggressive and aspirational vision statement that they still use today.

The ways that leadership communicates purpose matter greatly. What are the ways that communicate what a leader wants? Is the majority of an organization's official communication sent via email? Dr. DeBakey was relentless in connecting with people personally throughout the hospital, talking to them about their jobs and how what they did mattered in the greater scheme of things. To the janitor, he repeatedly emphasized the need for the hospital to be spotlessly clean to reduce the possibility of infection and showed genuine interest in how the janitor did his job. No doubt the conversations he had with the kitchen staff focused on the need for the food to be flavorful and appealing so people would want to eat it, thus nourishing themselves and speeding their recovery, and so on.

Going Beyond Transactional Communication

Leaders must be equally relentless in clearly communicating the purpose and must repeatedly use many different types of communication to ensure their intended message is received. The following are some of the methods of communication leaders can use beyond standard transactional approaches, recognizing that "receiving" is as important as "sending."

- **All-Hands Meetings:** These provide regular, consistent opportunities to communicate information and, wherever possible, field questions about ongoing operations and issues. To be successful, all-hands meetings must use full communication with a focus on both sending and receiving information, with ample opportunity for team members to provide feedback. Be prepared to potentially have some difficult—but necessary—conversations, and always ensure that the overall theme connects to the purpose.

- **Management by Wandering Around (MBWA):** While this method has been around for a while, MBWA sets useful examples for improved communication throughout organizations. Based on spontaneous interactions, MBWA encourages managers to engage in conversation to learn from these informal situations to aid in decision making, problem-solving, and more. Focus on relationship building, open communication, and communicating how the employees' everyday activities connect to the larger purpose of the organization to ensure that MBWA is not misconstrued as micro-managing or "watching over shoulders."

- **Skip-Level Meetings:** These should be used to get a qualitative feel for what people are experiencing on a regular basis. Done regularly, they can yield lots of information about employee views of purpose and their connection to it. At the outset, the people being "skipped" may be concerned that you are prying into their world or keeping tabs on them. The conversations should be wide-ranging and not necessarily limited to superior/subordinate conversations. As in the items above, this forum presents an excellent opportunity to help those attending see the ties between their work and the overall purpose.

What do all these suggestions have in common? Leadership must be willing to show that their people matter and what they do for the enterprise matters equally. When leaders show interest in the person, it is easier to help them discover the importance of their work. This lets the individual contributor connect their personal purpose and energy to the larger purpose of the organization.

Connecting to Purpose Matters

We repeatedly hear that people seek to become connected to something greater than themselves. How can this matter? The client I mentioned earlier that made an effort to change its vision statement landed in Crain's Chicago Business Top 100 Companies to Work For out of 14,000 entries. Connecting people's work to a larger purpose can return big dividends.

JJ's Takeaways

- People yearn to participate in something greater than themselves.

- Leaders must be relentless in communicating and connecting their team members to the greater purpose.

Part IV
Mission, Vision, Values

Culture Eats Strategy for Breakfast

—Peter Drucker

Edgar Schein, Emeritus Professor from MIT's Sloan School of Management, describes one of the key aspects of organizational culture as the artifacts that help articulate and clarify the culture for the members. Chief among those artifacts are the mission, vision and values of the organization. They are the most visible expressions internally and externally of the performance expectations for the enterprise. Many organizations not only communicate these to their members but also actively promote them on their websites and in marketing messages to the public.

Peter Drucker's oft-quoted comparison of strategy and culture rings true because strategy alone is not enough to create results. Every strategy requires robust execution to obtain the desired outcomes. The members' behavior within the organization is informed by the culture. A culture that is defensive and not adaptable stifles initiative and innovation. The best-crafted strategy that is poorly executed cannot produce the desired results. Leaders must relentlessly communicate vision, remind members of the mission and ensure that values are observed and upheld. These three vital artifacts form a stable platform for constructive cultures to form. Failure to ensure this platform leads to underperformance or, worse yet, destructive or criminal behavior.

Mission—Pointing the Way to True North

We're on a Mission ... from God.

—*The Blues Brothers*

Recently, I had the opportunity to tour two beverage packing plants. While I was touring the facilities, I would ask the floor workers, "What do you do here?" The answers varied a little from employee to employee, but at each plant, the answers followed separate themes. One group said, "We're making juice." At the other plant, the answers were grouped around, "We nourish people" and "We put smiles on people's faces when they're eating and drinking." Now, it is entirely possible that if you were to run a taste test between the two companies' apple or orange juice, you might or might not be able to distinguish them. However, I could easily point out the company that was getting better performance metrics all the way through to profitability outcomes. It was easy to see which group was engaged in what they were doing. What made the difference?

Engagement Matters

Are your people engaged? Do they understand the "why"? Actively disengaged employees alone cost the US economy $483 billion to $605 billion each year in lost productivity. According to a recent Gallup survey, these workers represent only 16 percent of the American workforce. They are clearly not happy at work and are a drag on improved performance. The productivity that we enjoy comes from the 33 percent who are actively engaged and those who are simply "not engaged." The sobering reality is that more than half of all American workers are "not engaged."

This poses a large risk and an equally great opportunity: Although they are available to be swayed to become engaged, absent clear, inspiring leadership, they can fall into the ranks of the disengaged. Given the compelling numbers demonstrated by those actively disengaged, management has a clear incentive to attract the members of the latter two groups to shift their mindset. A vital component of the effort needed to sway those from the "not engaged" and "actively disengaged" camps while ensuring continued engagement by the remaining 33 percent is a clear and compelling mission for the organization.

Dilbert is Right

In recent years, more leaders have grown their understanding of the impact culture has on an enterprise. As a result, mission statements have proliferated. The PR folks often spend hours crafting them. They have become so ubiquitous as to be sharply, and correctly, lampooned by the likes of Dilbert. In fact, go into any enterprise that has its mission statement on its website and see how many employees can actually recite theirs. Easy stock tip: Invest in those companies whose employees can. Simon Sinek, the author of *Start With Why*, talks convincingly about the reasons some organizations thrive, whereas others struggle just to keep up. He points out that successful enterprises are clear about the reason they exist long before they talk about how they go about it or what they offer. Mission statements, done right, help connect people to the purpose of the organization.

Pointing to True North: Good Business

A typical response for many to what an organization's mission is? To make a profit. In reality, profit is an outcome of properly and successfully pursuing what the enterprise has set about doing. Mission is what an organization does— every day. It should be compelling enough that it gets people out of bed and ready to go. In that sense, mission must point at the *Why*, the purpose of the enterprise. It needs to be aspirational in nature and provide leadership with a means to help connect the dots from the *Why* to the *What* and the *How* of an organization.

Mission is the organizational equivalent of a compass. By declaring its mission, an enterprise states the direction it expects to follow and, naturally, where its "North" is. The end result, its North Pole, then, is the organization's vision, usually characterized in a short, inspiring statement.

Whenever I visit leaders and talk about the value of strongly crafted mission statements, at some point, the following statement bubbles up: "Show me how this stuff moves the needle, then we can talk." According to Gallup, four in ten US employees strongly agree that the company's mission or purpose makes them feel their job is important. By moving that ratio to eight in ten employees, organizations could realize a 41 percent reduction in absenteeism, a 50 percent drop in hospital patient safety incidents and a 33 percent improvement in quality. Those kinds of numbers ultimately drive improved outcomes like those of the workers at the second packing plant.

Here are some well-crafted examples:

Honest Tea: To create and promote great-tasting, healthy, organic beverages.

Nordstrom: To give customers the most compelling shopping experience possible.

Vail Resorts: To create the Experience of a Lifetime for our employees, so they can, in turn, provide exceptional experiences for our guests.

Continuum Packing Solutions:
We transform your tastes into world-class products.

How They Did It

We talked with the leaders at the second plant to understand what created this kind of environment. They shared with us that they had pursued a steady plan of assessment, alignment, engagement and sustaining activity. They engaged in cultural surveys to understand the habits, attitudes, beliefs and expectations that existed within the plant and compared it with their vision of what they wanted them to be. They aligned their leadership by using diagnostics that provided insight into the leaders' mindsets and the impacts those mindsets had on the culture. When they had obtained acceptance of these insights by the leaders, they strove to engage the workforce by providing clarity through Mission and Vision statements and espousing the values they expected all to use to guide them in their everyday work. They spent time with the employees discussing the values and what it meant to them personally. And most importantly, they followed up—regularly reassessing to ensure that they remained aligned, making corrections as needed. Through this process, they developed trust, which fueled the mindset of all those at that plant.

Many enterprises take great care and dedicate precious resources to sharpen their external value proposition. If any of these issues matter to your organization, before thinking about how you go to market, be sure you have your internal compass set firmly and that everyone knows how to read it. Your employees will willingly take you there if they have a clear picture of the direction toward which they should be heading.

JJ's Takeaways

- Mission gives organizations a powerful compass.

- Clarity is a key to engagement.

- Mission Statements, properly executed, provide leaders with a powerful clarity tool to deliver high performance.

Vision—A Leader's Indispensable Tool

Start with the End in Mind.

—Stephen Covey

Vision: Churchill had it, Lincoln had it, Gandhi and Nelson Mandela, too. In each case, the outcome was not certain. Each faced monumental challenges; many might have concluded that there was little or no hope of success. At the outset, they did not know how they were going to realize their objective. Each would require time and tireless energy. None achieved their goal in the near term—all suffered setbacks and substantial criticism in the pursuit of their vision.

What was it? Each had the ability to envision a long-term outcome and communicate that picture in a compelling way so that people could see, believe in, hope and move toward that described future state. What made them stand out was the knack for articulating the broad view of that "state when fixed" that they had conceived and giving their supporters a way to realize where they could contribute.

The Right Stuff

In the 1960s, the United States was locked in a fierce ideological and existential struggle with the former Soviet Union. The atomic age cast a foreboding shadow over any interaction between the two superpowers. Missile technology was in its relatively early stages, and the Soviet Union had scored a series of early technological victories, the most vivid of which was the successful execution of the first human space flight, piloted by the Russian Cosmonaut Yuri Gagarin. In the background was the specter of the Soviet Union's ability to launch missiles with atomic warheads as payloads.

President John F. Kennedy realized that a compelling picture was necessary to channel the energy needed to bypass the Soviets and assure our well-being. NASA was in its infancy and struggled to deliver the required technological breakthroughs. In need of adequate funding, the agency requested resources from skeptical lawmakers. In a speech to Congress in 1961 endorsing this effort, Kennedy boldly established the vision that, "I believe that this nation should commit itself to achieving the goal that, before this decade is out, of landing a man on the moon and returning him safely to earth." In one simple, galvanizing declaration, this leader transformed the space race from two countries desperately struggling to weaponize a new environment into a noble quest of exploration and wondrous discovery.

It is naïve to think that Kennedy's speech defused the arms race; that race continued unabated despite his words. Nevertheless, the vision that he projected achieved two important goals. It shifted the entire focus from war and mutually assured destruction to one of seeking out new, unexplored places, something Americans had done throughout their history. Second, it captured the imagination of the members of NASA who would have the demanding task of actualizing his vision along with that of the voters who could easily conceive of the success of the mission and provided vital popular support.

What Kennedy and all these leaders did was to create a clear, compelling picture, and people were eager to contribute their unique talents in pursuit of that vision.

Vision Statements of Highly Successful Enterprises

To become the world's most loved, most flown, and most profitable airline. **– Southwest Air**

Our vision is to create a better every-day life for many people. **– IKEA**

Bring inspiration and innovation to every athlete* in the world. (*If you have a body, you are an athlete.) **– Nike**

A world without Alzheimer's disease.
– Alzheimer's Association

To teach others to become successful.
– Anago Cleaning System

Passionate People Inspiring Fruitful Ideas. **– Leahy-IFP**

Build the best product, cause no unnecessary harm, use business to inspire and implement solutions to the environmental crisis. **– Patagonia**

True North

In the previous segment (*Mission—Pointing the way to True North*), exploring the importance of the concept of Mission as a compass gave us a means of orienting organizations to focus directly on that which members should concentrate their energies. The pursuit of that daily focus, properly executed, should then lead the members toward attaining the vision.

To the Compass of Mission, Vision statements are the True North to which the mission points. Leaders use these two aspirational tools to help align and guide the members of an organization. They do it in alignment with the Values of the organization, which aid in decision-making. While we will discuss values later, we can see that, in this context, Mission becomes the "What"—which connects with Vision as the "Why," the overall reason for the organization's existence.

The Search for Purpose

This sense of purpose is a key driver in generating alignment within an organization. People yearn to be connected to something greater than themselves—and they want to know why they are being asked to do something. Most workers today, many of whom are millennials, approach a role and a company with a highly defined set of expectations. They want their work to have meaning and purpose. They want to use their talents and strengths to do what they do best every day. They want to learn and develop. They want their job to fit their life. Engagement results from the satisfaction that the work they do for an organization is meaningful.

This notion of meaning and purpose presents an enormous opportunity for many organizations. In the data revealed by the Gallup organization in its 2017 Study on Engagement in the Workplace, they found that:

- Only 22 percent of employees strongly agree the leadership of their organization has a clear direction for the organization.

- A mere 15 percent of employees strongly agree the leadership of their organization makes them enthusiastic about the future.

- Barely 13 percent of employees strongly agree the leadership of their organization communicates effectively with the rest of the organization.

Given these types of statistics, is it any wonder that only 33 percent of workers in the US are "Actively Engaged?" Organizations that are not performing among those statistics have a singular opportunity to create substantial improvement in traditional outcomes.

Another reason for vision is that humans are teleological beings: we subconsciously go toward those things about which we are thinking. Skeptical? Next time you are driving down the road, be sure to focus on the pothole in your lane and see what happens!

According to Professor Emeritus John Kotter, Harvard Business School, Kennedy's genius was in providing a vision that was critical for vision statements: Imaginable, desirable, feasible, focused, flexible and communicable. Creating a powerful vision for an organization not only charts a powerful destination toward which its members can actively strive, it sharply frames the value proposition that it seeks to deliver to its external audience as well.

JJ's Takeaways

- Vision provides leaders a tool for organizational alignment.

- When paired with Mission, Vision creates intense focus.

- A sense of purpose engages an organization's members, producing improved outcomes.

Values—Guard Rails for Alignment and Execution

*It's not hard to make decisions once
you know what your values are.*

—Roy Disney

Organizations do well when they establish a Mission and craft a Vision. Mission spells out clearly what it is we do. Vision vividly outlines and connects us to the purpose of the Mission. However, they do not stand alone. Having a Mission and a Vision is akin to blowing up a balloon (Mission) full of air that propels us to our destination (Vision). Once we let go, what happens? Absent some guidance, the balloon could fly in any direction.

Values act as that guidance system. Vision informs us about where we want the balloon to go. We use Values to regulate how much air to release and when; values act as the guidance fins to harness the air at just the right speed to drive us toward the True North of our Vision.

Values then, are the concepts by which organizations can reliably guide their decision-making and actions. Values initiatives have nothing to do with building consensus—they are about imposing a set of fundamental, strategically sound beliefs on a broad group of people. What values organizations elect to follow—and how well they adhere to them—fundamentally informs the culture and how people are expected to think, act and behave in order to fit in and perform well.

Balloons, by their nature, can be delicate; it is important then that the guidance system not be overly elaborate. Values should therefore be simple, straightforward, easy to communicate and implement. And not too many...

Values Require Backbone

Committing to strong values—and sticking to them—requires real guts.

When properly practiced, values can inflict pain. They may make some employees feel like outcasts. They limit an organization's strategic and operational freedom and constrain the behavior of its people. They leave executives open to heavy criticism for even minor violations. And they demand constant vigilance. Misused, they lead to apathy and disengagement.

The noted writer about organizational behavior, Patrick Lencioni, describes Values as falling into certain distinct categories: Core, Aspirational, Accidental and Permission to Play (table stakes).

Core values are typically extremely limited in number, and members would likely endure some adverse consequence or punishment rather than violate them. History recalls that Sir Thomas More was Henry VIII's Chancellor. In the play *A Man for All Seasons*, More is challenged by a young zealot about doing what it takes to achieve his aims, including breaking long-established legal precedent. More responds by asking the young man if he were pursuing the devil through a dense forest, would he chop down all the trees to get at him?

Naturally, the young man replies that he would.

Then, More asks the young man, "suppose you chopped down all the trees and in chasing Satan, you came to the sea and He turned on you … where would you hide, the forest now gone?"

More went on to explain that the law was like the forest. He chose adherence to the law as one of his core values. We know that More lost his life rather than violate that core value. Although this example is rather unusual, it frames the concept well. Unfortunately, it clashed with Henry's core value of preserving the Monarchy at all costs, including taking More's life.

Naturally, this is an extreme example. In business, people are rarely willing to give up their lives. Two business stories highlight how espoused values became a clear indicator of the integrity of the culture and the organization.

In the 1990s, Enron was a high-flying, dynamic organization that was the darling of corporate America. The Houston-based company at its height boasted over 22,000 employees. Within a short span, the company had spiraled out of control and declared bankruptcy in 2004. In May 2006, a jury convicted Enron's Jeffrey Skilling of nineteen counts of conspiracy, securities fraud, insider trading and lying to auditors. In his role as CEO, he maintained a facade of success as Enron's energy business imploded. For his failure, he was indicted, convicted and sentenced to twenty-four years in prison.

In its annual report to shareholders, Enron listed its core values as follows:

1. Communication – We have an obligation to communicate.

2. Respect – We treat others as we would like to be treated.

3. Integrity – We work with customers and prospects openly, honestly, and sincerely.

4. Excellence – We are satisfied with nothing less than the very best in everything we do.

An example of their failure to uphold their highly publicized values was the behavior of its CFO and Board Member, Andrew Fastow. To continue to build revenue on Enron's balance sheet, Fastow undertook an elaborate process of establishing special partnerships to bundle assets and secure loans. Understanding that Fastow's involvement in these partnerships was a violation of its code of ethics, Enron's board voted to suspend the code of ethics' application to Fastow while these partnerships were active! Other employees, witnessing this type of behavior, followed suit to disastrous consequences. The failure to honor their values caused the "guidance fins" on the balloon to malfunction, thrusting the business into insolvency.

By contrast, Southwest Airlines has a simple set of values. Its late CEO, Herb Kelleher, exemplified a steadfast commitment to upholding them. A frequent flyer nicknamed Pen Pal, the type of customer that represents the holy grail of every airline, habitually sent detailed complaint letters to the management at Southwest. Her last letter, reciting a litany of complaints, momentarily stumped Southwest's customer relations people. They bumped it up to Herb's desk with a note: "This one's yours."

It took only sixty seconds for Kelleher to pen a response. The note said, *Dear Mrs. Crabapple, We will miss you. Love, Herb.* In one brief note and swift action, the CEO firmly upheld the value Southwest's Servant's Heart: Living the Golden Rule, treating others with respect and embracing the Southwest family. With this type of insistence on a core value, their balloon has high functioning fins on its fully energized balloon, whisking them safely and securely as they strive to become the world's most loved, most flown and most profitable airline.

> ## Group 1: Live the Southwest Way
> - Warrior Spirit
> - Servant's Heart
> - Fun-LUVing Attitude
>
> ---
>
> ## Group 2: Work the Southwest Way
> - Work Safely
> - Wow Our Customers
> - Keep Costs Low

Hope is Not Enough

Organizations often espouse what they believe is a core value, but they ignore the consequences upon their violation. Although not flouted as in the Enron incident, these are more likely aspirational values to which a company truly wishes to uphold but fail to do so consistently. For example, a company adopts the value of respect. However, employees at all levels are routinely late for meetings or multi-task during them. They believe that they respect one another, but that isn't really happening. The fact that they waste people's time because they deem another task more important suggests that respect is not one of their real values.

More likely, the culture has created an accidental value that, in order to "get things done," over-scheduling and attempting to do two things at once are viewed as acceptable. In fact, when making decisions about timeliness, the accidental value is the determining factor. These accidental values come into being because of real behaviors within the organization. Running late becomes the norm, disrespecting those who made an effort to be on time and prepared.

The espoused value may look good as part of an external value proposition, but internally, it churns time and reduces engagement, costing the organization in several areas. Tasks take longer to complete, people experience burnout, causing mistakes and delays that affect product delivery and customer service. These not only impact people within the business but can also have a direct effect in terms of brand and consumer confidence in the enterprise.

Values declarations today, like mission statements, are ubiquitous; 80 percent of the *Fortune* 100 tout their values publicly—unfortunately, these values often stand for little but a desire to be perceived as mainstream or, worse still, politically correct. Empty values statements create cynical and dispirited employees, alienate customers, and undermine managerial credibility. "Permission-to-Play" values simply reflect the minimum behavioral and social standards required of any employee. They tend not to vary much across companies, particularly those working in the same region or industry, which means that, by definition, they never really help distinguish a company from its competitors.

55% OF ALL *FORTUNE* 100 COMPANIES
CLAIM INTEGRITY AS A CORE VALUE,
49% ESPOUSE CUSTOMER SATISFACTION, AND
40% TOUT TEAMWORK.

An organization's Mission and Vision can create tremendous energy and the potential for movement. An effective guidance system, carefully considered Values, provides the members with a clear understanding of what is advisable and useful to guide their behavior and decision-making in pursuing their objective. How well leaders ensure adherence to these values contributes largely to the resulting outcomes of profitability, engagement, quality, retention and safety. Leaders who insist on choosing their values carefully, match their internal and external value propositions, and have the courage to follow through can look forward to a healthy culture and strong, sustained growth.

JJ's Takeaways

- Values inform decision making as we pursue our Vision through our Mission.

- Values are vital as a guidance mechanism for Mission and Vision.

- Organizations develop different types of Values – Some are more effective than others.

- Values assist leaders in developing clarity of purpose for the organization.

Part V
Mindset

In the fixed mindset, everything is about the outcome. If you fail—or if you're not the best—it's all been wasted. The growth mindset allows people to value what they're doing regardless of the outcome. They're tackling problems, charting new courses, working on important issues. Maybe they haven't found the cure for cancer, but the search was deeply meaningful.

—Carol S. Dweck, PhD

Is the glass half empty ... or half full? Long before people discussed mindset, this phrase separated most people into two large tribes. How they look at life has a major impact on everyday performance and, by extension, in the workplace. Organizations, by their nature, establish goals that can often be difficult to attain. Mindset can contribute materially to achieving personal and professional objectives. How we look at things can make it easier or harder to see the way through.

Inside each of us, we have a "clue-finder" that researchers and physicians refer to as the Reticular Activating System. It is a series of fibers wrapped around the brain stem that act as a filtering mechanism. We use it to screen out information that is unimportant to us and makes sure we are aware of information that we consider important or a threat to us. Our beliefs about what is or isn't important help train our "clue-finder" to turn up information that helps us keep safe, solve problems and create solutions. In short, our beliefs control the information we receive.

Thomas Edison repeatedly failed in his effort to create a working light bulb. After one of his many failures, his lab assistant is said to have asked him why he wasn't discouraged at the large number of times they were unable to break through. His response was simple: "That's so many times that I don't have to worry about anymore." As we know, he persevered and found the proper filament. What was his mindset? Surely, we can see that he believed that he would find the right solution. His "clue-finder" stayed active, giving him cues and clues that guided him to the solution. What do you think would have happened if he believed that "there is no way?" We would probably be celebrating someone else for the invention of the light bulb.

Leaders must adopt this "growth mindset" and be tireless advocates for liberating beliefs over limiting ones. They must use that mindset to help them find ways to equip their people to grow and flourish.

The Simple, Compelling Power
of Liberating Beliefs

*We behave and act, not in accordance with the truth,
but with the "truth" as we believe it or perceive it to be.*

—Lou Tice

Two different people with the same talents, skills and competencies, one succeeds, the other does not—why? They both work hard, neither cheated; what took one over the line and not the other? Often it is what is inside the mind that matters. Much of what we believe determines whether we limit or liberate ourselves in our performance. As leaders invest in their organization's internal value proposition, they have the opportunity to envision and support liberating beliefs among the members.

Henry Ford Was Right

Henry Ford once said, "whether you believe you can, or believe you can't, you're probably right." Belief is a powerful tool that can enhance or inhibit performance. A classic case of this was a group of students who participated in a standardized test at the beginning of the school term. When the teachers received the results, they assigned the children to groups based on their scores. Predictably, the group with the higher scores progressed faster and obtained better grades than the other groups throughout the year.

There was only one problem: the students in that "upper" group had actually scored <u>lower</u> on the original test than the other children! The teachers were completely unaware. It was they who were the real focus of the experiment. With these expectations developed in the minds of the teachers, they acted on their liberating beliefs in the abilities of the "upper" group and instructed those students in a way that delivered better results.

Sadly, they also taught the others in a way that fulfilled the teachers' reduced expectations of their "lesser" capacity. Consequently, those children progressed more slowly and obtained lower grades. The limiting beliefs from these "Who Said's" about that group's abilities trapped those students and effectively hampered their progress. At that age, children often accept opinions from others as the "truth."

In this case, so did the teachers.

If this story is any guide, leaders can leverage this process for the good of an organization and its employees, creatively deploying the power of liberating beliefs to help improve performance and employee engagement. A key Leadership responsibility is Connecting the Dots for those responsible for implementation. Good leaders find a way to help their people envision a way that they can successfully perform a task, even when they are in unfamiliar surroundings.

FEDEX: A Poor Idea?

Maintaining one's liberating beliefs in the face of a "Who Said's" limiting beliefs is equally important. Fred Smith is the CEO of FEDEX, a company that disrupted the entire parcel delivery industry. While he was a student at Yale, he wrote a term paper that outlined what such an organization could become. The professor, apparently unimpressed with the concept, gave the paper a poor mark. He could easily have sanctioned that professor's limiting belief. Undaunted, Smith later implemented his vision that he created in college. After serving in the Marines in Vietnam, he founded the company that has become a $70+ billion global transportation, business services, technology, and logistics company serving more than 220 countries and territories.

Fuhgeddaboudit!

I was able to witness this effect on a more personal stage. Many years ago, I worked as a ski instructor at the Copper Mountain Resort in Colorado. One winter, we'd been blessed with early snow, and the resort opened in advance of the Thanksgiving holiday.

Late that Wednesday afternoon, I had just finished a private lesson and was enjoying the sun on the beginner hill when I heard a noise that sounded a little bit like a crow's caw. I looked around and saw very few people on the hill. Again, I heard an "aaaawkk" sound. This time, I saw a tiny person at the very top of the lift, motionless. When I asked her what she was doing, she told me she was warning people to stay away from her! It seemed odd, but she was rigidly braced, poles jammed in place in the snow. Naturally, I asked her if she needed any help, and we managed to get her to the bottom in one piece.

Since this area on the hill was reserved for lessons, I asked her where her instructor was. Crestfallen, she replied, "She left me." When I asked why she said, "She told me I should forget it. I could never learn how to ski." I was astonished. Here was someone who had paid good money to a professionally certified instructor in order to be able to pursue a goal that she wanted and risked being thwarted by her guide's expression of a highly limiting belief.

We agreed to meet first thing the next day. As we got our gear on, she shared with me that she had come with her son, who lived in Dallas with his family, to spend the Thanksgiving holiday. It turned out that she was eighty-four years old, recently widowed and wanted to be able to spend time with her grandchildren on the mountain. She was deeply disappointed to have traveled all the way from her home in Cincinnati to Texas and then to Colorado, only be told to give it up.

As we talked further, I learned that she had studied at the Sorbonne in 1933 and had taken classical dance classes there. She was tiny, five foot four, and wore a size 4 boy's hiking boot, and she was game.

Plié—Relevé

The solution was simple. What she needed was to connect the dots from her days as a dancer to what she needed to do as a skier. Instead of giving her the doctrinaire advice for ski technique, all it took was to ask her to execute a simple *plié*, the classic ballet move in which the dancer bends her ankles and knees in a graceful dip.

That single movement gave her control over her feet and thus her skis. After that, she found her rhythm, sliding safely and gracefully (albeit slowly) down the gentle slope of the bunny hill. She understood she was never going to become Lindsay Vonn (the world's winningest ski racer). All she wanted was to share time with her family, who were crazy about skiing. She just needed someone to help her "see" her way to the goal.

One leader said, "You can't." Another said, "When you can see it, you can do it." A leader's ability to create a picture connecting belief to their people's actions frees them to tap into their capacity to perform. For the most part, people want to contribute and do well at their work. The only thing this delightful lady needed to attain her goal was to see how her competencies related to her current challenge. As with many types of leadership exchanges, I did relatively little but affirm her belief in her own capacity. Through her creative genius, she discovered the "how."

That Saturday, with the breathtaking view of the Rockies as a backdrop, a diminutive eighty-four-year-old widow shared a bucket-list family lunch at a mid-mountain restaurant and made her way happily back down because someone helped her see her potential realized. As a leader, what mountains will you move by simply nurturing liberating beliefs in your people? Leaders who invest in this kind of enhanced value creation in their people tap into the tremendous potential that young and old alike thrive on realizing.

> ## JJ's Takeaways
>
> • Leaders' ability to help others adopt a growth viewpoint is key to generating higher performance.
>
> • Inner beliefs have a strong influence on actions.

Milestones Matter: The Celebration that Adds Value Beyond the Bottom Line

Come on feet don't fail me now
I got ten more miles to go
I got nine, eight, seven, six
I got a five more miles to go
Now over the hill just around the bend
Huh... although my feet are tired, I can't lose my stride
I got to get to my baby again

—Edwin Starr

Organizations with constructive cultures celebrate milestones. Here's why: Doing so drives better performance.

Efficacy

Dream Teams at the Olympics are a relatively novel phenomenon. Before allowing professional athletes to participate in the Olympics in more recent times, all the athletes were expected to be amateurs. The Winter Olympics, held at Lake Placid in 1980, featured a collection of upstart college kids from all over the country to represent the US in hockey.

Their coach, Herb Brooks, had succeeded in guiding his young athletes through the qualifying rounds and into the knockout medal rounds. To win the gold medal, they had to defeat the mighty team from the Soviet Union, arguably the best hockey team on the planet.

Brooks saw the potential in his athletes and spent the run-up to the Games shaping them both physically and mentally to be ready for this single encounter. In the locker room prior to the contest, he coolly pointed out that they were made for the moment at hand and that they had the capacity, in this one special instance, to be able to prevail against a distinctly superior opponent.

Although he may not have known it at the time, he was referring to the concept of efficacy, in this case, the team's collective efficacy. Normally used in describing how well a medical treatment or a course of pharmaceuticals is working, the term took on new meaning when Professor Albert Bandura of Stanford University used it to describe a person's belief in their ability to bring about or cause something to occur.

He went further to suggest that people do not necessarily operate at their level of capacity but at their level of belief about their capacity. It follows then, that people tend to self-regulate their performance at their belief level.

Brooks succeeded in elevating the team members' sense of efficacy to the point that they pulled off a "miracle," defeating the Soviet team in the semi-final round and going on to defeat Finland for the Gold medal. He found the way to cause his team of under-experienced college players to find the belief within themselves of what they could accomplish on the world's highest stage for athletes. It remains to this day one of the great expressions of what self-belief can accomplish against staggering odds. The conversations that these athletes had with themselves and within the team must have been enormously affirming.

Research tells us that we experience between 60,000 and 70,000 thoughts in a day. When people act, performing a task at work, for example, their thoughts will lead them to behave in accordance with their belief about their ability in that specific function.

We hear these kinds of thoughts expressed out loud all the time, "Oh, I'm not particularly good at sales," or "I just don't do well with new apps on my phone." Consequently, when they see themselves perform the task, they will evaluate their performance based on their opinion of their efficacy immediately after the action. If they perform to their expectation, they tell themselves, "Yes, that's like me to do it that way." They offer themselves that thought to confirm their self-appraisal, thus reinforcing their belief in their level of efficacy. It's a very virtuous, complete cycle; it serves to confirm their belief in the type of performance they expect from themselves.

Conversely, if instead, they perform more poorly than they expect, their appraisal of that act sounds more like, "No, that's NOT like me!" Once again, by offering this thought to measure against their established belief system, they subconsciously set about correcting for the "mistake" of under-performing. In the case of poor performance, this kind of self-regulation can also be a virtuous cycle because it helps us correct ourselves when we fail.

The problem is that this type of correction also occurs when we perform *better* than we expect. When that happens, we set about correcting in the other direction so that we once again find ourselves snugly cosseted within our zone of expectation. Compounding this problem is a tendency most people possess, says Professor Bandura, in which they pass too quickly through their successes and dwell too long on their missteps. Thus, any improvement in performance that might influence our beliefs gets less weight in our minds than our shortcomings.

Spiraling to Higher Performance – Using "Self-Talk" to Enhance Efficacy

There is a way out of this "Goldilocks Effect" we experience in performance. Leaders must strive to help build the efficacy of their people. When they succeed, members raise their own expectations to a higher level. It follows, then, that if leaders want to see better performance, they must go about building that higher sense of belief in the members' improved, and very real individual capacity.

An important component of this is setting clear, challenging and achievable objectives for people to strive toward. Because the objectives are achievable, they can be measured. In the case of annual turnover, progress can be measured weekly, monthly and quarterly. Project implementation, progress in innovation, profitability and efficiency: all of these can likewise be quantified.

Just as we can quantify goals, we can also foresee key

achievement points along the way to the target. In attaining a milestone, organizations provide themselves with the opportunity to celebrate movement toward the objective. Acts of recognition energize the self-talk assessment cycle described earlier and provides leaders an opportunity to emphasize that it is "like us" to attain and visualize these tiers of success.

Repeating this recognition through self-talk, the members sanction the thought that leaders offer. It provides them a chance to begin to build and, with repetition, reinforce the collective efficacy of the organization, thus raising their appraisal and belief in what they can accomplish. As this cycle continues, it reduces underperformance and stretches the capacity of the members of the organization. Stretching capacity makes the previously "unrealistic" come within reach.

The Shape of Water

What should these celebrations look like? They can be big or small, whatever is appropriate to the moment. Avoid generalities—they should be specific and inclusive. While it can be okay to recognize one or two individuals, most organizations require levels of teamwork to function well. Even a concert soloist needs the orchestra to underpin the work that is most visible.

Milestones, then, are a way of confirming and elevating our capacity and our efficacy. They are a way of energizing the members to perform at the level of their potential by "catching them doing things well."

The Gallup organization regularly performs a nationwide assessment of worker engagement in the US. Their results reveal that those workers who believe that the work they perform matters are substantially more engaged and productive than those who are unclear about their impact. According to Gallup, only three in ten employees working in the US strongly agreed that in the last six months, someone had talked to them about their progress. By moving that ratio to six in ten employees, organizations could realize 34 percent fewer safety incidents, 26 percent less absenteeism and 11 percent higher profit.

Milestones matter. Affirming and strengthening an organization's sense of internal value strongly enhances a constructive culture. This confident sense of efficacy empowers the members to exercise their tremendous external competitive advantage in today's marketplace.

JJ's Takeaways

- Efficacy, a reflection of beliefs, controls behaviors, thus determining performance.

- Organizations need to invest in growing members' efficacy.

- Milestones provide important inflection points in the effort to build efficacy.

Uncertainty Can Leverage Innovation

In the midst of every crisis, lies great opportunity.

—*Albert Einstein*

Crisis Creates an "Amygdala Hijack"

Crises turn our lives upside down. 9/11, the global financial crisis in 2008, political upheaval are all examples. The Covid-19 pandemic was another. As with the others, it disrupted our lives in a myriad of ways. The majority of us led out-of-the-house lives, chock full of public appearances, multiple commitments and high expectations.

Most of that came to a screeching halt, except for the expectations. It is easy to see why the pandemic left us feeling trapped, restless, frustrated and fearful. From an organizational perspective, it put a premium on enhancing capacity to help keep teams focused and productive. With all the issues swirling around in people's minds, that can pose a daunting leadership challenge. Understanding what is going on inside can provide some hints for effective solutions.

It is no secret that people prefer to operate in an area where they have a positive expectation of success in the actions and tasks they pursue. People are inclined to stay with the known, the familiar. Gestalt psychologists contend that the human mind is constantly seeking order.

Habits become a way of establishing those patterns of order. We repeat activities until they become familiar to the point of "unconscious competence" as a coping tool. We become accustomed to a certain level of performance within this set of habits. As long as we remain in this space, give or take a certain acceptable plus or minus factor, we operate calmly, comfortably and unconsciously.

This "comfort zone" is easy to spot. For instance, whenever a large new effort is mounted in IT, it shows up immediately. Try telling people they must use new software or a new app on their smartphone and watch the general reactions. Changing schools, doctors, banks; all these disruptions tend to take people beyond their comfort zones. They display discomfort, sometimes becoming irritable and unhappy. People often resist adopting these new approaches. When implementing these changes in a corporate setting, performance inevitably suffers, at least temporarily.

There are normally three classifications for comfort zone analysis that change management practitioners recognize. In the central sector of this zone, Goldilocks, everything is expected, the outcome is known and actions are on "autopilot."

In the adjacent Stretch area, the person may not know the outcome but likely has a positive expectation of success and, thus, is possibly willing to briefly extend beyond "Goldilocks," perhaps permanently if successfully repeated.

The final area is beyond the pale of positive expectation and causes discomfort and resistance. When the mind perceives that the situation is too alien for a sense of comfort, there is an effort to "get back to Goldilocks." If this Danger zone is judged too extreme, the resistance can be visceral, and the mind reacts with ancient, instinctive protective behaviors. In this space, the reaction can be immediate and without regard to normally accepted behaviors.

As with other crises, the existence of Covid complicated the comfort zone scenario in a wrenching fashion. The daily bombardment of threatening information about the virus and its devastating effects triggered authentic feelings of fear that reach our minds' safety and protection centers. Deep inside the oldest part of our brain, an area called the Amygdala is constantly scanning for threats. When something penetrates too deeply into our psyche and we perceive ourselves to be in the Danger zone, the Amygdala is activated and the well-known "fight or flight" mechanism takes over.

Danger
• Negative Expectancy   • Amygdala Hijack

Stretch
• Outcome Unknown   • Positive Expectancy

"Goldilocks"
• Automatic   • No Learning

Unfortunately, the Amygdala is not located in the part of the brain where language operates. When this "Amygdala Hijack," a term coined by Daniel Goleman, occurs, the mind operates exclusively on emotion and deeply embedded instincts for preservation. Because this area does not contain language, it can be very difficult to use reason to settle someone engaged in the fight or flight reaction. Logic and reason are not available when we are in this situation. When this happens in an organizational context, team members are literally not listening and will not until the hijack is brought under control.

What can leaders do to facilitate this process? Watch any retail commercial. Advertisers do everything they can to inject the concept of "safe and secure" into their product pitches. For leaders, this means not only ensuring the safety within the physical plant the organization occupies, but leaders must also pay extra attention to their members' emotional stability.

It is imperative that team members have a chance to reset from the Amygdala Hijack before attempting to restore focus on an operational level. This requires substantial legwork on an Emotional Intelligence level before anything else can be approached. Giving team members the time and space to voice their concerns, helping establish a sense of order in this new, unaccustomed space, will yield solid benefits and enable organizations to move forward effectively. In effect, leaders help their team members create new comfort zones within the existing framework.

It may be challenging to get the members all the way to "Goldilocks" in this environment, but once leaders have helped their team members shift their mindset to "Stretch," they can move toward helping their teams thrive in this new environment. We will examine ways to approach this in the next segment.

JJ's Takeaways

- Understanding comfort zones provides insight into team member productivity.

- The "Amygdala Hijack" blocks performance.

- Leaders can help members reset to prepare for innovation.

Winding the Coil: Innovation in Difficult Situations

*Crises and deadlocks when they occur have at least
this advantage, that they force us to think.*

—*Jawaharlal Nehru*

Crises can create paralysis. When negative inputs become
too overwhelming, our "Fight or Flight" reactions can also
create a third option, "Freeze." Unfortunately, when people
act in any of these fashions, innovation and performance
suffer. Leaders have difficulty moving their organizations
forward when their team members are in the throes of an
"Amygdala Hijack." Earlier, we discussed comfort zones
and their impact on our performance. When we experience
major displacements from our comfort zones, such as the

threat of Covid and the restrictions imposed, performance can plummet. What must leaders do to respond to this?

The first step is to reassure team members and give them the ability to unwind from their defensive postures in which they operate uniquely on emotion and instinct. They must be able to reconnect to language and logic before they are able to listen, think and interact constructively. Leaders need to assuage these feelings by tapping into emotions associated with successful, rather than fearful, actions. They need to help their members tap into their resilience and capacity to deal with challenging situations. Often this can take the form of connecting them with something they achieved and/or overcame in the past. Authentic recognition of their legitimate safety issues helps remind them of the leaders' concern for them personally as well as a member of an organization.

As leaders work to help their team members return from the Danger area far beyond their comfort zone, it might be tempting to think that getting them fully back into their "Goldilocks" level would be desirable. In fact, good leaders can capitalize on the uncertainty created by the crisis to help catalyze innovation and higher performance. Although it may seem counter-intuitive, allowing team members to cocoon themselves in their most comfortable place would be counterproductive.

Comfort Zones Suppress Meaningful Change

Gestalt psychology holds that humans constantly strive for order in our minds. Consequently, we cannot hold two opposing thoughts on a topic simultaneously without tension, also known as dissonance, being created.

Think about people who are "compulsive picture straighteners." When they walk into a room and discover a picture hung improperly, it bothers them. In fact, they will often immediately adjust it, even if it is in a public place or someone's office or home. If they cannot, they will agitate until they cause someone else to handle the issue. Until the picture is "fixed, repaired, set right," they struggle to focus on anything else.

It is that dissonance that leaders can harness. The mind always resolves the tension of two clashing ideas in favor of the dominant image and does not rest until that difference is eliminated. In the case above, the notion of a straight picture is indelible and clearly dominates the person's thinking. In the same way, comfort zones are usually extraordinarily strong mental image markers or boundaries. As such, when we move beyond them, we often become uncomfortable and seek quickly to get back where we are at ease, returning our world to "order" as we know it.

The opportunity created by a crisis is that our "now" has already been disturbed. Leaders leverage this by creating and relentlessly communicating vivid, energizing future pictures and ideas—"BHAGs" (Big, Hairy, Audacious Goals) that create sharp dissonance between the familiar now and the new objective until those new visions become more compelling.

By deliberately throwing things "out of order," just as with the case of the crooked picture, enterprising leaders create the dissonance that they can resolve in favor of the newer, more dominant image. The uncertainty of our current situation itself generates the opportunity to energize a decisive move forward rather than retreating to the former comfort zone or remaining in the unsettling "now."

Earlier, we described using our Clue-Finder to help us find solutions. Leaders succeed in stimulating innovation in team members when they paint a vibrant, vivid picture of the contemplated outcome and connect to the positive emotion associated with achieving that outcome. This creates a pathway for people to move beyond the crisis thicket, avoid the Amygdala Hijack and break through to innovative solutions designed to achieve the vision they have created.

To recap: When team members are thrown out of their comfort zone because of a crisis, it is vital to acknowledge their feelings, recognizing that they may only be operating on emotion and instinct. When the members demonstrate that they have returned from that extreme state, leaders can capitalize on team members' return to the Growth (Stretch) area, providing graphic, compelling visions for future action, clearly spelling out the "why." In this fashion, leaders can stimulate healthy creativity and help boost performance in their team at a time when others are simply trying to put the former picture back into place.

JJ's Takeaways

- Step One – Ensure your team members are out of "Amygdala Hijack."

- Comfort Zone dynamics aid leaders in stimulating innovation.

- Leverage dissonance, imprinting a compelling future picture that is stronger than the "now."

- Vision vividness and clarity anchor the pathway to innovative solutions.

Part VI
Engagement/Satisfaction

He who has a why to live for can bear almost any how.

—Friedrich Nietzsche

Employee engagement is uppermost in the minds of most forward-thinking business leaders. They are acutely aware that only two or three people rowing in an eight-oared scull are not going to generate a lot of speed. Better to have all eight putting their full weight into the project.

In the United States, the chief chronicler of this phenomenon is the Gallup organization. They routinely publish reports about the state of engagement among employees in this country. The information they deliver creates a fair amount of energy and contains actionable recommendations. In recent years, they have come to understand that systems that operate within an organization, chiefly its culture, are responsible for the level of engagement that Gallup so accurately measures.

Leaders have a disproportionate impact on culture. If an organization has less than satisfactory engagement, it is up to the leaders to shift behaviors so that their members embrace engagement. They need to understand the primary desires employees have to achieve satisfaction from their work.

Spoiler alert: It isn't non-stop coffee and snacks or ping-pong tables, although these artifacts can contribute to the overall culture. Viktor Frankl, the noted Viennese psychiatrist and Holocaust survivor, believes that humans seek meaning in their lives. It is this search for meaning within their lives and fulfilling it that leads to self-actualization and what we might call satisfaction. Through this effort, employees become engaged in the work that they do. Leaders who bend themselves to assisting their team members on this quest will reap the benefits of their most creative labor.

Leadership is a Level 3 Activity

A group of people get together and exist as an institution we call a company so they are able to accomplish something collectively that they could not accomplish separately – they make a contribution to society, a phrase which sounds trite but is fundamental.

—David Packard

The Declaration of Independence famously enshrined "Life, Liberty and the Pursuit of Happiness." But what does that mean in organizations? And how does leadership fit in?

Attracting good talent is expensive—losing it is even more so. One of leadership's main challenges is to create an environment in which team members thrive, perform well and feel validated that their work matters. Employee satisfaction surveys consistently report that people leave an organization not for money but because of their immediate supervisor. Employees want an environment where the work they do is challenging and meaningful. Although money matters, it's the satisfaction that keeps them happy … and working productively.

Distilled to its essence, leadership is the ability to get other people to accomplish things for the leader's purpose. There are many ways to do this; however, not all of them leave the team members happy and satisfied. And, there are many types of happiness. Leaders who find the sweet spot in delivering the right levels of satisfaction and happiness produce superior results. Leaders who focus on winning—being on top—may get results, but they will not be sustainable, and it will cost them in terms of turnover, productivity, mistakes and rework.

Plato's Four Levels of Happiness

What does happiness mean in an organizational context? The word can have many different definitions. In fact, 2,500 years ago, Plato used four different Latin words to differentiate types of happiness.

Level 1 Happiness – Immediate reward, intense, short-lived. If we walked by a bakery and saw and smelled a chocolate chip cookie, then ate it, that would be Level 1 satisfaction/happiness. An hour later, you might want another one.

Level 2 Happiness – Reward is not always immediate, can still be powerful, and is somewhat longer-lasting. Level 2 is characterized by the emergence of the ego, being "Better Than." It's the satisfaction of achievement. When we win a game of chess or a big contract, run faster than, jump higher than, sell more than, etc. The winning may take more time, be important to us and the feeling may last longer. Typically, though, it is a zero-sum, win/lose proposition. Also, the pay value of repeating the prior win has diminishing returns, requiring bigger and bigger wins to obtain a similar level of happiness.

Level 3 Happiness – Reward can take longer to develop, but the satisfaction lasts longer; however, it is not nearly as intense. Level 3 is characterized as being "For the Good of." When we help someone solve a problem, learn to walk, talk, think, communicate, help them attain a goal, etc. It is a win/win proposition.

Level 4 Happiness – The reward can be characterized as a sense of Ultimate Truth, Ultimate Beauty, Perfect Execution—although this satisfaction is rare and fleeting in experience and very low in intensity, the impression of happiness/satisfaction can last a very long time. An example of this might be the appreciation of a remarkable sunrise or sunset. The beauty is infinite, as is the memory of it.

"Better Than"

In organizations, most individual contributor behavior is predicated on Level 2 activity and rewards. Sales personnel are evaluated on their ability to sell more than the prior year. Accounting team members are valued for their improved accuracy and speed in gathering and reporting the information. Lawyers are recognized for their ability to litigate better, obtaining better settlements and judgments. Unfortunately, some of this can be internally focused. Sales personnel performance is often ranked, one salesperson versus the others. In that environment, it can be difficult to stimulate team collaboration.

"Good For"

Leaders are often lionized for being high achievers, as being "better than" others who have performed in similar positions. By contrast, leaders should concentrate on behaviors in the Level 3 area, focusing on "good for" behaviors for their team members. Leaders should be in the business of helping create an environment in which their people can thrive in their Level 2 pursuits. The leaders' satisfaction comes as they help their reports connect to a larger purpose and discover the best ways to achieve their performance objectives.

Enlightened organizations also help team members connect to a greater purpose which typically also yields a Level 3 reward. By helping their reports succeed well in their duties, they are working "for the good of" their team members. In the envisioning process (annual and strategic planning), leaders should be thinking in terms of the "good" of the organization in setting objectives toward which the enterprise intends to thrive. Then, as execution comes into focus, leaders should naturally seek to inspire their people to contribute to the success and aligning them for maximum productivity.

While attaining the outlined goals may produce a Level 2 happiness in terms of organizational performance, great leaders derive that much longer-lasting Level 3 happiness from the development of their people in how they approach issues and problems and resolve them. When leaders use these types of expectations and rewards, they deliver more effectively for their organization; a true win-win.

JJ's Takeaways

- All four levels are valuable to humans.

- Leaders, and employees, must adjust their expectations based on the level being pursued.

- When thinking about "Better Than," "Good For" isn't a consideration – and vice versa.

- Purpose and Meaning are the foundation for "Good For" performance.

Employee Satisfaction—The Right Measurement for Engagement?

Research indicates that workers have three prime needs:
Interesting work, recognition for doing a good job,
and being let in on things that are
going on in the company.

—Zig Ziglar

Employee satisfaction surveys abound; should they?

We see post after post about employee engagement and articles that describe how important it is to have the right perks so that workers will be happy at work. Companies lavish workers with programs and offerings to retain employees because they perceive "it's a fun place to work." If that is the case, why do Gallup's recent Engagement surveys report that of the roughly 100 million full-time employees, only 33 percent are described as "Engaged?" While world-class organizations generate engagement in 70 percent of employees, the rest are struggling with "Actively Disengaged" or "Not Engaged" workers. What sets them apart? One thing is certain: Measuring workers' contentment is not an effective way to deliver improved business outcomes.

What causes high-performing enterprises to generate such an improved level of engagement? They have established the habits, attitudes, beliefs and expectations that create satisfaction, meaning and repeatable success. Called "Organizational Culture," these commonly accepted ways of doing things in order to fit in effectively determine the behaviors and decisions of the members and thus its performance.

The leaders in these organizations recognize that they have accepted the challenge to mentor and grow those responsible for the tasks required. They understand that there is dignity in work and that people want to know that their work is meaningful. When team members realize that, they choose to become accountable for their work. They become actively engaged.

Employers who seek to create "happy" environments are focused on the climate (not the culture) within the organization. They attempt to create an environment in which work-life balance issues are addressed. Or, they create an atmosphere within the workplace that is energizing, pleasing, comfortable. So, we see workout facilities, yoga classes, ping-pong tables, snacks and other happiness perks. These are admirable steps, affect the internal "Net Promoter Scores" and generate high marks in satisfaction surveys. Establishing a proper climate is important. Unfortunately, climate can be highly transitory.

Leaders come and go. A new leader may come on board and announce, "We need a new culture here, and I am authorizing the following steps immediately." This is followed by the initiation of some of the programs mentioned above or other climate-shifting efforts. The leader's efforts gain traction, and climate scores rise. Unfortunately, despite the uptick in happiness and possibly better reviews on Glassdoor, it doesn't necessarily translate into more traditional outcomes, productivity and profitability.

What happened? Although the leader declared the desired culture change, the efforts produced only climate changes. The underlying behaviors that people are implicitly expected to display were not affected. So, although the leader engaged in well-meaning efforts, absent the culture changes underneath, real performance will remain the same. The climate changes will likely disappear with the leader's departure to a different post or company.

I live in a part of the States where we only get nine inches of rain a year. Immediately to the east, it rains even less. An hour's drive in that direction leads to a highly productive farming region renowned for its alfalfa and melons. Yet, both crops require far more rainfall water than the region normally receives on average. In wet years, there might be enough water. In dryer years, the crops would wither, hostage to the fickle climate of wet vs. dry.

So how do they do it? They use a permanent irrigation system that takes advantage of the snowfall that accumulates in the mountains to our west. The runoff, stored in reservoirs, provides a steady flow of water to the region and a prosperous farming community. Even if the climate changes and the area experiences a drought period, which happens occasionally, the irrigation system, channeled through the water from the reservoirs, maintains the crops.

What maintains performance or improves it in organizations is culture. The leadership that invests the time and energy to develop a robust "irrigation" system of mission, vision, values and purpose will yield consistent performance and a "climate" of success. Climate is an outcome of culture, not the other way around. When a good culture exists, or leadership moves to install one, the efforts at climate are embraced as a confirmation of the culture.

Enlightened, high-performing organizations invest relentlessly in culture and track it continuously. Only then will their efforts in terms of climate yield meaningful results. At my company, Level Three Performance Solutions, we have capably shown leaders the impact of their culture on their current results and where the opportunity lies for exponential improvement.

JJ's Takeaways

- Surveys to improve satisfaction generally only measure climate.

- Climates can easily change, without culture underpinning.

- Climate is an outcome of culture. Start with culture first.

Part VII
Leadership Communication

Developing excellent communication skills is absolutely essential to effective leadership. The leader must be able to share knowledge and ideas to transmit a sense of urgency and enthusiasm to others. If a leader can't get a message across clearly and motivate others to act on it, then having a message doesn't even matter.

—Gilbert Amelio

New engagements always require extensive pre-work. Before I begin with a client, I hold a series of Appreciative Inquiry style listening sessions to determine what's going well and what needs bettering. In my thirty plus years as a management consultant, I have yet to go into a listening session in which the client told me that communication was perfect and needed no additional work. Instead, there are concerns about how to message externally to reinforce the brand; how to message internally to improve engagement, spur creativity, strengthen accountability.

At Disney's theme parks, cast members are never allowed to be seen out of full uniform. They are keenly aware of the message they send to their customers and to each other. Leaders should take note. There is not a moment in the workday when a leader is not "on stage" performing a most important role. Each thing a leader does results in a form of communication to everyone involved.

The leader's challenge? What have my audiences heard from what I have intended to say?

Leaders need to spend time reflecting on where the enterprise is going. They also need to reflect on how their messages should communicate and how well that is accomplished.

Five Strategies for Leadership Success

When people are financially invested, they want a return.
When people are emotionally invested,
they want to contribute.

—*Simon Sinek*

Every new year promises to provide great opportunities. The road to success, while open, is often littered with challenges—downturns, huge new customer acquisitions, supply chain miscues, shortages, innovation breakthroughs, competitor disruption, mergers. Amid these and other threats and opportunities, leaders need to be able to move their organizations forward. The challenge is often the same: Plan and execute calmly amid turbulent surroundings. Here are five strategies that can be employed immediately and throughout the year to ensure success in your organization.

Build Your Team's Efficacy

As a leader, you may think you are responsible for getting things done. While that is an outcome against which you are measured, in fact, as a leader, your real responsibility is to the <u>people</u> who actually execute the tasks that result in the deliverables you are expected to provide. In other words, you can't get all those things done by yourself; you have to rely on others to do them for you. If they are not energetic, organized and focused, those outcomes can be less than desired.

What would it look like if your team members were optimistic, growth-oriented and accountable? These are the kinds of behaviors that determine their efficacy, what they believe they can bring about or make happen. And because they are engaged by a leader whom they are confident is interested in their own growth and helps them relentlessly pursue possibilities, they are highly likely to seek accountability and responsibility for their task area.

Pursue Clear Goals

When the people for whom you are responsible have a high-definition understanding of what is expected of them, it creates an atmosphere where they know what to do and can deploy their efficacy to the best advantage. Leaders want to stimulate proactive, innovative, future-oriented behaviors. Help them visualize what success looks like. Use mistakes that occur as opportunities to improve, focusing on what to do the next time. To encourage creativity and innovation, invite them to challenge assumptions to achieve better results and try new approaches to improve performance. Once you have provided clarity on the goals, encourage them to plan the execution and ask probing questions on the desired outcome. Then, it's time to tell them to shove off, make things happen and engage in their own minute course corrections along the way. When we first went to the moon, the capsule was only on course 20 percent of the time.

Ensure the Proper Approach

Your team members are looking to you for cues—clues and encouragement to inform their behavior. The examples you model are as important as the words you use. They will be well guided by your behaviors of excellence, integrity and transparency. It is important to communicate the "why" along with the "what." Modeling excellence, constantly striving to improve, raising the bar are all qualities you must insist upon. That will require of you a consistent level of integrity. This means acting on your convictions, expressing your ideas even when they are unpopular, and always staying within ethical bounds. And you must expect and encourage the same from your team. Transparency and crystal-clear communication are a must.

Build Relationships

An organization is a team: helping teammates appreciate their contribution to the overall effort engages and empowers them. Good leaders foster the power of positive regard among teammates, emphasize teamwork and find effective ways to mentor others.

Building a team means appreciating the talents and contributions your contributors can make. A whiff of judgmental activity on your part divides your team members and sends them into list-making and comparing themselves against each other instead of focusing on the challenges at hand.

Take the time to listen to the hopes and concerns of your teammates, which will encourage them, in turn, to do the same with their people. As their mentor, it is important to share tips to help your people become successful and actively celebrate their successes.

Focus on Altruism

Great leaders help those around them connect to the larger purpose of the organization. They exhibit and foster gratefulness, humility and a sense of greater purpose. They are acutely aware that information can come from anywhere and that they will respond positively when recognized for their contributions and those of others. Because of this, when you are open to ideas that differ from your own, you encourage others to develop broader-based thinking. Most importantly, people will naturally work for their own self-interest. When you succeed in helping them connect to the higher purpose of the organization, you free them to grow independently because they are aligned, without conflict, highly engaged.

The road to exponential growth is open. These five strategies, pursued diligently, will drive the culture of your organization, energizing the members and producing the kinds of outcomes that will withstand the uncertain winds along the way.

JJ's Takeaways

• Keep these five strategies on your dashboard at all times.

• Take time to reflect on your progress and plans.

• Seek feedback often, be open to course corrections.

Avoiding the Pitfalls of Leadership Communication

We must expect to be misunderstood. We must expect to misunderstand.

—Kenneth G. Johnson

The distinguished Professor Emeritus from Wisconsin and noted communications specialist made this assertion long ago. If this is true in everyday communication, difficult times magnify the problem. Consequently, leaders need to be sensitive to the things their team members are listening for when we communicate.

As a leader, you may decide to upgrade efficiency. This can include shuffling some people around, putting people in better "seats on the bus" to improve performance. Because humans are wired to pay attention when things change, they will be tuned in when you communicate about those changes. The problem is <u>what</u> they are thinking about when you propose these changes.

Dr. David Rock created the SCARF model to help describe the kinds of communications that can stimulate hyper-vigilance in people. Leaders must be mindful of their message because what people hear may easily overshadow the leader's intended meaning. Long before they can process the features and benefits of the proposed reorganization, team members are likely to run through a bundle of (typically) unasked questions. When team members hear these messages, their "threat surveillance system" scans for clues and cues that can imperil their situation or help them move forward. Dr. Rock's model describes five areas of particular emphasis.

Status – Do I still have a job?

Certainty – What do I need to not fail?

Autonomy – Will Big Brother be snooping?

Relatedness – Does everyone have this problem?

Fairness – Will my contribution be noticed?

People are concerned first about their STATUS—will mine be affected, diminished in any way? How will other people perceive it? Any whiff of a reduction in status will create defensiveness and justifications. At that moment, the team member on the receiving end stops listening and immediately begins formulating reasons why the change shouldn't happen. Any potential benefits evaporate in the face of the passive resistance that will surely follow.

The next category is one of CERTAINTY – Am I clear on what I am expected to do? People want to know what they need to do to succeed and what is necessary to avoid failure. Ambiguity or confusion leads to uncertainty and hesitation on the part of the team member. In today's competitive world, the last thing organizations need is to slow down execution because the leader failed to provide clear expectations.

Following that is AUTONOMY – If I am clear on what I am supposed to do and I have the necessary skills, will I have the room to do my job on my own or will someone be breathing down my neck, "sweating the money?" Nothing triggers our threat surveillance radar faster than micro-management.

The proposed changes will also cause them to seek RELATEDNESS – how will this affect the rest of my team? Is this something that will benefit the team and we can all support? Something that doesn't consider the team as a whole will cause additional resistance.

Lastly, is there a sense of FAIRNESS – Is this just for a short-term personal gain or is it connected to something greater than themselves? Studies have repeatedly shown that team members respond more constructively when they can feel connected to something larger and that their contribution is to a larger purpose. A positive example of this occurred when Winston Churchill needed to present grim news to his country and said to them, "I have nothing to offer but blood, toil, tears and sweat."

Armed with this awareness, leaders can craft their message so that they address these concerns. If the proposed change does indeed fall afoul of one of these items, the leader must take the time to explain the "why" and make a compelling case. Most people are willing to deal with negative news if there is a reservoir of trust that the leader has built up. Further, s/he must be impeccably straight with the receivers about the situation and its reasons. If the change can be a plus for all, it is particularly important to cover each of the items clearly so that team members can see and understand the benefits. Covering these issues first enables the leader to move to the features and benefits of the proposed change in a way that all can listen and focus on the objectives presented.

Good news or bad news, whenever leaders seek to create change, especially in challenging times, it is particularly important to think of Dr. Rock's SCARF model to ensure that the message is properly received.

JJ's Takeaways

- SCARF deploys directly on top of the Strategies of Efficacy, Clarity, Approach, Relationships and Altruism.

- Use SCARF to create a Growth Mindset in your team members.

Leading Your Army from Their Living Rooms

Five Ideas for Maintaining Business Sanity in Today's World

... Ain't nothin' gonna break-a my stride
Nobody gonna slow me down, oh no
I got to keep on movin'

—Mathew Wilder

Leading "BC" (before Coronavirus) was relatively straightforward: Get the troops together, talk about where the enterprise is headed, share assignments and say, "Off you go!" Since then, for a majority of organizations, it's become a little more complicated. According to Gallup's engagement surveys, the global pandemic merely accelerated a trend that was important for organizations to incorporate in their regular order of business in order to thrive. This is not a new phenomenon. Global organizations have operated within distributed environments for quite some time now. In a more hybrid environment, what can leaders do to help keep things moving forward and create a heightened sense of stability? Here are five points leaders can use to create an effective replacement picture for the one people experienced in the former brick-and-mortar only workplace.

- <u>Maintain a Daily Rhythm</u> – Your team members now operate either in two places for performing their daily duties or one completely distributed one. Help establish a stable framework by creating a regular (daily, biweekly) Stand-Up meeting that gets everyone on the same page in terms of issues and priorities regardless of their work location. Everyone can check-in for their specifics either during the meeting or at individual communications following. Find a time that works best for your business and takes into consideration the reasonable timing for all.

- <u>Be sure to "Make Face"</u> – Today's technology gives leaders an enormous edge in maintaining personal contact. There are many video-conferencing apps and services that you can employ to be visible with your team members. Leaders should take every opportunity to make personal level connections to help their people stay connected to their purpose. This can be employed in the daily Stand-Up as well as with individual connections.

- <u>Ensure Clarity</u> – In general, clarity leads to engagement. In today's environment, clarity is even more vital as the workforce is dispersed, and it can be difficult and time-wasting to correct when a problem is discovered later. Use the Stand-Up to ask for team members to restate what they believe they have been assigned to accomplish. In that way, they clearly delineate to the leader what accountability they are taking. If there is a misunderstanding, the leader can adjust the message and clarify during the meeting or off-line following.

- <u>Celebrate Successes</u> – The Daily Stand-Up can be used to celebrate victories achieved by team members. By starting off the meeting with "What Went Well" in preceding days, the team begins the cycle on a positive, energizing note which helps propel them into their work. The added bonus is that later in the meeting, leaders can focus on "What We Can Do Better" (not What We Did Wrong), and it provides for constructive guidance.

- <u>Build Trust</u> – Because team members are working in diverse environments, they may allocate their time differently than if they were in an office environment. Smart leaders give them the freedom and responsibility to execute what is expected within their own time construct. When your people do this, they choose to be accountable, and you build trust within your organization. Engagement soars within this environment.

When you create a picture that your people can easily see and rely upon, they will integrate themselves more quickly and effectively into this evolved environment. Be present for your people, and they will respond well.

JJ's Takeaways

• Create a cadence your team can rely on.

• Now, more than ever, it is impossible to overcommunicate on key issues.

• Trust creates engagement – go the extra distance in a distributed environment.

Part VIII
Clarity = Authenticity = Honesty

I said speak your mind, Jack, but Jeez!

—Adm. James Greer, The Hunt for Red October

The pace of change continues to accelerate at a tremendous rate. Organizations must innovate or risk finding themselves disrupted, possibly irrelevant in today's race to improve. We have discussed the need for leaders to inspire others to contribute their creative genius in the pursuit of the organization's purpose. In *The Five Dysfunctions of a Team,* Patrick Lencioni considers the freewheeling debate over ideas and concepts that an enterprise is considering as essential for high performance. We have talked at length about the need for leaders to explain the "why" along with the "what" to ensure clarity. Members of the organization must have the ability to ask frank questions and expect direct answers to fully understand what is expected of them in order to succeed.

This can only occur in an organization with a culture that encourages its members to challenge assumptions regularly. Leaders must value and recognize team members who speak their minds, ask penetrating questions and consider alternative approaches to problems and solutions. Many, perhaps most, breakthrough solutions occurred outside of the customary pathways that people would use to solve issues or approach problems.

This kind of organization can be difficult to manage, but the results are usually worthwhile. This means that there must be a high degree of trust within the organization.

People must believe that the items brought forward are intended to improve the organization and its members and is not done for personal aggrandizement. Members must be tolerant of far-fetched concepts and be willing to engage in discussing them. Responses to these kinds of proposals need to be "Yes, when the following can be resolved..." instead of "No, because..." The people within the organization must believe that their contributions are worthy of being voiced and that they are in fact delinquent if they hold back.

All of this requires a culture that values contribution and creates an environment that encourages participation. Three key qualities must exist: engagement, integrity and psychological safety. These ingredients create the foundation for innovation and exponential growth.

Engagement, Integrity and Psychological Safety

Once you become the Archbishop, you never get a cold meal… and you never get the whole truth.

—*Timothy Leahy*

Is that true in your organization? How much of the real story gets to the executive suites? How much of what is coming down from leadership is accurately relayed to and heard by the folks doing the work? Great cultures have the knack of flowing communication up and down the entire operation with limited distortion and filtering. The result is high performance and employee satisfaction.

Why does this matter? In a word, Engagement.

What does engagement feel like? It is the simple perception by team members that "the work I do here matters." When people believe that "I understand my role—what I say and do is important to the enterprise," communication flows, productivity soars, as does retention, workplace safety and innovation.

Simple, right? Easy? Maybe…What do leaders need to do to foster and enhance this type of environment?

Organizations have minimum requirements below which people are no longer permitted to work there. Show up on time, provide a certain quantity of deliverables, play well with others… The challenge is that while this form of "appropriate excellence" (just enough to stay below the radar) may permit a company to survive, it is far below what is needed to thrive in today's competitive marketplace. In other words, to achieve an organization's goals, team members must be willing to volunteer their vast creative genius to bridge the gap between the minimum requirements and the standards for excellence.

Leaders must rise to the challenge of helping workers engage and connect. They have the responsibility to assure "flow," a sense that the team is executing without friction and in a state of high concentration and collaboration. As organizations become more physically dispersed, team members can find that it is more difficult to engage with one another. In a distributed environment, impromptu hallway conversations disappear. To encourage socialization, leaders need to link workplace strategies with social technologies and work policies.

Socialization has other requirements. Team members must have high integrity and be willing and free to say what they think. In fact, many of the so-called "meetings after the meeting" exist because some are unwilling to express themselves fully within the original gathering. In this context, it is easy to see that psychological safety is not at an acceptable level.

Every organization seeks to develop among their employees the notion that they display high commitment, energy, and, above all, integrity. But that's the point, isn't it? Just as two-thirds of all licensed drivers believe they are above average drivers, an overwhelming majority of employees claim that they have high integrity. Despite what they believe about themselves, scores on culture assessments often reveal lower than desired integrity ratings. This is often attributable to the fact that people judge themselves on intent rather than actions. Leaders have the obligation to create the proper, psychologically safe environment to foster true integrity within the culture.

There are several items that comprise integrity. Beyond the universal concept of "retaining one's personal integrity," there are other areas that deserve notice. How many times has someone "stared at their shoes" in the moment instead of saying something contrary or controversial only to hear from that same person their true opinion in informal conversations after the meeting concludes? How much time and productivity gets lost in this type of asynchronous communication?

Do employees actually do what they say? How often is doing "whatever it takes" misinterpreted as to go to extreme lengths, regardless of morality or legality, to achieve the desired result? Whose agenda and values get trampled in this kind of environment? Fear is the controlling factor here.

How Often Do You :

Act on your convictions

Express your ideas/concerns even if they are unpopular

Retain your integrity

Realize that the ends justify the means

Just agree with others to fit in

Do whatever it takes to get the result

THE BLUEPRINT TOOLSET™
The Pacific Institute ©

Leaders who succeed in creating clear expectations, connect people to the larger purpose of the organization, and relentlessly model the values they expect to see followed can expect to participate in an environment where people feel comfortable to speak their minds. When they do, they develop the greatest opportunity for flow and high performance within their organization.

Sustaining psychological safety requires constant attention. It is a mindset that must be cultivated to empower interpersonal risk-taking. Psychological safety is the *why* behind our responses to the questions, "Can I speak up? Will I be punished or ridiculed for sharing my opinion?

Can I be honest about who I am and my perspective?" Leaders and team members need to alert themselves to conditions that lower or raise interpersonal fear. Because we are experiencing a time in which issues of equity, diversity and inclusion take center stage, leaders must recognize that psychological safety contributes to a culture that promotes integrity and thus engagement.

In the final analysis, engagement is an outcome of culture, which is informed by the levels of integrity throughout the enterprise. Encouraging a climate of psychological safety creates the opportunity for integrity through high communication flow. It is a winning combination well worth the effort to sustain it.

JJ's Takeaways

- Engagement is an outcome of culture.

- Integrity is a key component of culture.

- Leaders must ensure psychological safety, reinforcing integrity.

Have to? Or Want to?

*No work is insignificant. All labor that uplifts
humanity has dignity
and importance and should be undertaken
with painstaking excellence.*

—Dr. Martin Luther King

There is a radio station in my town that has an aggressive ad campaign to attract listeners. In it, they sport a raft of testimonials from current listeners about how the music they play helps them "get through their day." Many of the speakers clearly convey their sense that their work is a drag, something they "have to get through." They claim that the music the station plays helps them take their mind off their work. When leaders seek to help keep their team members' minds on their work, this can pose a problem.

Typical workers? Maybe … Engaged? You be the judge.

The American workforce had more than 100 million full-time employees in 2017. One-third of these are what Gallup reports as "engaged" at work. They enjoy their jobs and make their organization and America better every day.

At the other end, 16 percent of employees are "actively disengaged"—they are, at best, grudgingly and reluctantly present in the workplace and impede and degrade what the most engaged employees have built. The remaining 51 percent of employees are simply "not engaged"—they're just there, taking up space, resources and time, getting through the day.

The productivity differences that exist in organizations between the average (33 percent engaged) and world-class (70 percent engaged) are startling. Gallup's study is brimming with eye-popping comparisons that contrast the two. Knowing this, how come so many workers fall into the category of those who struggle to make it through the day? Sadly, it is because their organizations have failed them.

Wait a minute! Don't organizations pay their wage, provide them with training, benefits? Help me understand how the organization has failed them?

In a word: Culture.

Culture is defined as a series of norms through which people are implicitly expected to think, act and behave in order to fit in. Typically unwritten, the members pass on these norms in the ways that they interact. So, culture can be described as:

- The way things are done here.

- When leaders are not present, the culture informs others about the actions and decisions they may or may not make.

- Real culture emerges when the organization is under pressure or deadlines.

- It is the "glue" that holds the organization together.

Think back to those folks in the radio commercial. They would likely self-describe that they "have to" do their assigned tasks. What would it take to flip that "have to" into a "want to?" What if leaders thought more deeply about the ways these workers view their tasks? Do they see what they do as meaningful, worthy of the dignity Dr. King refers to above? Probably not. Thus, having concluded that their work isn't meaningful, it is easy to see that, in order to obtain their paycheck, they "have to" complete their assigned tasks. The culture clearly communicates to these workers that their work isn't meaningful. Consequently, it is easy to see how they are "not engaged." What do you think their productivity would be given this mindset?

Other organizations invest in their culture and help their workers understand the value that they add to the overall purpose that the enterprise seeks to fulfill. Because they are connected to the underlying purpose of the organization and know the "why" behind the "what," the employees within this culture easily understand and appreciate that their work is meaningful, freeing them to fully engage their capacity to contribute with all their energy and creativity. Because their work matters, they "want to" perform their assigned tasks. It would be easy to conclude that these employees have become "engaged." Productivity and performance follow as a matter of course.

Organizations that foster a culture of "mattering" enjoy the fruits that come with engaged workers. Almost any outcomes measure would reflect that difference: from safety, attendance, innovation and productivity all the way to profitability. When organizations transform their culture from one of paycheck to one of purpose, the enterprise rises easily to a higher plane of performance.

The moral of the story? Investing in the inherent dignity of work and the people who perform it yields the engagement that seems otherwise elusive. When the culture is right, engagement naturally follows.

JJ's Takeaways

- "Mattering" is important for engagement.

- Engagement occurs as an outcome of consistent culture cultivation efforts.

- Highly engaged organizations share common philosophies and practices.

Integrity—A Key
Component of Culture

*In a room where people unanimously
maintain a conspiracy of silence, one word
of truth sounds like a pistol shot.*

—*Czeslaw Milosz*

Imagine sitting in a meeting of peers, discussing a new way of scheduling workflow. Your group keeps getting interrupted by another department's urgent requests, and the result is that work you have committed to previously is not getting done in a timely fashion. As a result, your team risks missing its objectives and being adversely judged. The group settles on an approach to balance the team's pre-determined tasks with the interruptions from the other department.

The plans your team discusses focus on prioritizing your pre-determined work over the urgent interruptions by other departments because your team's recognition and rewards are based on achieving your original planned output. By contrast, you personally believe that in order to help the organization overall, it is important to accommodate the other departments. The team is strongly in favor of the proposed workflow solution. What do you do? Just agree? Persist in your approach?

Later, your manager convenes a meeting of the group to discuss its lag in producing outcomes as agreed earlier. She wants to know what the group intends to do about it. Your team presents its new workflow approach to her that prioritizes departmental goals first. She says that it is important to accommodate the other departments first and then asks for input. What do you and the rest of the team say? Do you support the team? Your leader?

In your production facility, safety is considered the most important factor. Your production managers have created a program for promoting safety awareness using suggestion cards. Their intent is to cause every team member to be alert at all times for ways to improve safety in areas large and small. When a shift submits a threshold number of suggestion cards that have been signed off by the supervisor in a given month, the entire group qualifies for a bonus.

At month's end, an audit of the suggestions submitted reveals that only a small number of employees on the shift actually provided the cards that achieved the target. The cards were signed off by the lead on the shift, not the supervisor. All of the suggestions were valid. One of the submitting members is also on the plant-wide safety committee. Were they just "doing whatever it takes?"

The finance department notices that cash flow is unusually low at month's end. One of the covenants of the organization's bank loan requires a certain level of cash flow in every month. The Controller uses an accrual account to convert a journal entry into cash, relieving the pressure on the covenant. The accrual account can be replenished in the coming cash-heavier months.

What happens next in each case is largely determined by the culture.

If we were to ask any of those employees, "Do you retain your integrity?" The answer would likely be an overwhelming "yes."

One of the major facets of culture is how well distortion-free information moves up and down within an organization. Is it timely, meaningful, credible and actionable? Often, the movement of information in an organization is heavily dependent on the integrity of the senders and receivers. In each of the situations above, there is a potential conflict that needs to be resolved. In the first instance, should the team member speak up about how s/he feels about the workflow? Or keep quiet in order to preserve team harmony? What do the organization's values promote? Harmony over innovation? Freewheeling debate or consensus overall? An enterprise that leans toward suppressing debate will likely see only "safe" ideas or the possibility that the train runs off the track before anyone raises the alarm.

When the team's manager presents an entirely alternate view, what do you and your team members do? If the leader fails to encourage discussion and thoroughly discuss the "why" before settling on a course of action, the team gets the message that their input isn't really welcome, and communication slows down.

In the case of the safety suggestions, it is likely that management was looking for broad-based participation in the program. Does the communication from leadership (the bonus plan) drive people to fulfill expectations while possibly bending ethical limits? Recognition and reward programs are a critical way for leadership to communicate what is valued within the culture.

In the cash-flow case, how important is it to stay within the covenant? Would communication with the bank about the situation and how the enterprise is expected to rectify it serve? Are there other solutions? Or does the end justify the means?

All of these situations require integrity. Leadership must be relentless in communicating, supporting and living by the values the organization truly embraces. Otherwise, they risk placing their members in positions that create tension in terms of real integrity. Previously, we discussed creating an environment of psychological safety. That space provides members the ability to retain their integrity. That environment only exists when the culture empowers its existence.

Organizations that want to do more can track the isues in their culture that matter. These cultural components are easily measured.

JJ's Takeaways

- A majority of people believe they have high integrity.

- Culture determines levels of psychological safety.

- Strong culture prevents integrity conflicts.

Safety Fosters Innovation

I prefer to be true to myself, even at the hazard
of incurring the ridicule of others, rather than
to be false, and to incur my own abhorrence.

—Frederick Douglass

Innovate or Die? Today's disruption comes from organizations and their teams that took the risks to innovate.

What stimulates innovation? A culture that prizes proactive behavior, appropriate risk-taking and engagement across the enterprise. What makes this type of climate possible? Psychological Safety. Leaders who create this environment have a leg-up on fostering exponential growth.

Patrick Lencioni's well-known leadership fable, *The Five Dysfunctions of a Team*, takes a deep dive into the best practices for improving organizational performance. In his book, the author paints the picture of a leadership team that engages in constructive improvement commentary among the members as a group. In it, the group members openly share with each other what they believe other team members need to do to optimize performance.

In today's world, these types of constructive improvement conversations can be very risky. As Lencioni notes, such conversations cannot succeed unless there is a strong level of trust among the members. Ego, coupled with an aversion to being perceived as less competent or making mistakes, makes executing these exchanges properly very difficult. Leaders must foster a mindset among the members that welcomes the information as an opportunity to improve, not as singling someone out for competitive criticism. When teams operate in this fashion, it is what Michigan State's Head Basketball Coach Tom Izzo refers to as a "player-coached team." This takes time and repetition; the payoff is worth the effort.

What can leaders do to create such an environment? They must develop a climate of psychological safety. Members need to believe that they can wholeheartedly contribute without being ignored or criticized—to be able to take risks and admit mistakes. This is a vital component that must exist deep within a company's culture to create an environment of innovation and growth.

Organizations that emphasize "being right" or "making no mistakes" run the risk of shutting down psychological safety. In this setting, perfect is certainly the enemy of the good. Interestingly, these kinds of organizations usually report fewer mistakes in their operations. That statistic, however, can be illusory. It may well be that people are unwilling to acknowledge errors for fear of retribution or shaming because of the lack of psychological safety.

Amy Edmondson, Novartis Professor of Leadership and Management, Harvard Business School, found in her research on teams in hospitals that charge nurses who were judged by their teams as being better leaders often had higher rates of documented errors than those who were reported to be inferior leaders. The increased error reporting reflects the sense of trust in their leaders and the space they provide for them to take risks and admit mistakes in order to learn and improve from them.

Today's competitive environment requires all the collective genius teammates can muster. Organizations require innovation and proactive thinking from everyone in the enterprise. If they do not have the psychological safety to advance unconventional thinking, the business model risks being disrupted by more forward-thinking competitors in the market.

What creates this sense of safety? Language, followed by action that matches. Previously, I discussed Dr. David Rock's SCARF model. When communicating with others, leaders need to be alert to five key areas: Status, Certainty, Autonomy, Relatedness and Fairness. Using this approach, leaders can focus on areas that are of key interest to team members and their security.

Another factor in creating an environment of safety and trust is authenticity in leadership. A key attribute of authenticity, according to Lencioni, is vulnerability. It is the foundation for the creation of trust. Leaders who demonstrate their willingness to be vulnerable encourage others to do likewise and thus build psychological safety.

Leaders need to be role models for what they expect to see in others. There are some simple ways in which a leader can signal vulnerability. One is acknowledging and owning mistakes. Another is in how feedback is handled. In his book, *What Got You Here Won't Get You There*, noted executive coach Marshall Goldsmith counsels simple strategies for acknowledging a mistake: Say, "I'm sorry, I'll do better next time." When someone provides constructive feedback: Say, "Thank you." No more, no less. By acknowledging one's errors, a leader encourages and models the type of behavior that is expected. By acknowledging the feedback without necessarily giving it sanction, the leader encourages honest and open feedback and displays continued vulnerability as well as being open to alternate ideas. Repeated to the point of habit, these kinds of trust-building actions become embedded in the culture. Consistent application of these approaches will aid leaders in developing the proper climate.

JJ's Takeaways

- A player-coached team stimulates improvements.

- Trust is the foundation for psychological safety.

- Innovation relies upon well-focused, risk-taking strategies.

Epilogue
Resilience—Gratitude

You don't miss your water... 'til your well runs dry.

—William Bell

Every year presents us with crises. Earthquakes, fire, terrorism, hurricanes, riots, economic disaster, sickness and death—where does it all end? When people get to the end of any year, many will surely be ready for a beer or a glass of wine, maybe two.

In any given year, people worldwide are faced with extraordinary circumstances. Often, these disasters are met with equally extraordinary levels of compassion, humanity and ingenuity. If there were two words that characterize this, they would be Resilience and Gratitude.

Somehow, though, people seemed to pivot, shift themselves and carry forward, albeit some better than others. A poignant example of this was the Coronavirus pandemic. People who could, continued to work—from their living rooms or the spare (or kid's) bedroom. Overnight, an entire country found out what they could do with video communication software.

One of my clients was in the food business! Kiss of death, right? What did they do when their manufacturing and packaging orders fell off the table? Hand sanitizer seemed in short supply. And just like that, because they had a very constructive, nimble culture, they transformed their business model to respond to the needs of the moment.

A consulting company that I work with had historically delivered all of its education via live facilitation. In freefall, they successfully made the transition to an all-virtual presentation format within sixty days. In addition, they began presenting entirely digital modules.

In the middle of the chaos, another client and friend found himself in the ICU with a triple bypass and clots in his lungs and his leg! Not exactly elective surgery! This friendly giant of a man faced his own greatest existential threat. He has mended and is happily contributing again.

There are hundreds of these types of stories. My business relied on face-to-face coaching and consultation. And while Zoom worked wonders to present much of the work that I do, I found that everyone I met was hungry for the sense of community from which we had been deprived by that ugly virus.

What did everyone who has moved forward have in common? Grit…resilience. They bounced back from what could have been a whole series of crushing blows. They found a way to improvise, adapt, even thrive.

The enterprises that have done this best are, unsurprisingly, those with the most constructive cultures. They did as they have always done: rallied their people, were as transparent as possible, clear in their expectations and relentless in terms of preserving their values in the face of unnerving pressures. They had unshakeable faith in their mission and purpose, staying focused despite the challenges swirling around. And they believed that even though the solution may not have been immediately apparent, they had the tools and the drive to capitalize on it when it appeared.

We see this over and over. A snowstorm paralyzes a region; an earthquake destroys a major city; tornadoes destroy crops and homes; a disaster visits an entire community. In any of these situations, the one thing that is so evident is how grateful people are for all of the help and comradeship displayed by complete strangers. The resilience that so many display, picking up the pieces and beginning again. The cheerful patience of everyone as they learned to navigate a novel landscape—our family, our friends, our good clients and stakeholders.

Resilience is a hallmark of efficacy. It is also a key component in the framework of a growth mindset. We see it every year in the people around us. Leaders need to continually reinforce this evident sense of grit and resilience that we see in the challenges our team members face every day. By appreciating it all around us, we remind ourselves that it exists within everyone; all we have to do as leaders is to help them realize it in a meaningful fashion.

JJ's Takeaways

- Resilience and grit are the children of efficacy.

- Efficacy, like muscles, needs a regular workout – in others and in ourselves.

- Gratefulness brings a calming spirit to our troubled lives – take full advantage.

- People and organizations have unending potential – we see it every day. Leaders help them tap into it by helping them change their thinking.

Acknowledgements

There are so many people for whom I am grateful. La Vonne, my wife of thirty-four years, has been present every day in a thousand little ways, steadfastly believing in me. My sons, James and Patrick, encouraged me to pursue my passions. Compiling this kind of information takes time and a team. My sister Sarah, ever the inquisitive one, reviewed my work and prodded me to be better. Her husband Paul was kind enough to create line art, much of which grace these pages. Artwork, design and thoughtful counsel have come from Bill Egan and his team at Trungale+Egan, a superior marketing firm in Chicago. My publisher, Calumet Editions, took a chance with me when others were reluctant.

In the field of leadership, I owe so much to many. First among them is Gaston Perrot. He didn't know it at the time, but he taught me about efficacy, envisioning and mindset. All he thought he had done was hire a laborer. Chuck Lewis was the head of the Copper Mountain Resort. He gave me my first insights into the workings of a CEO. Pat Cruzen and Michael Georgilas, best and worst CEOs I ever served under respectively as a senior leader. Lou Tice, as founder, and Joe Atteridge, Chairman of the Pacific Institute, awakened in me what is possible in transforming leaders and their organizations. Michael J. O'Brien, and through him Drs. Clay Lafferty and Rob Cooke, demonstrated the tools that could validate what could happen when applying my skills and training well with clients.

As for my writing, if you have enjoyed this book, I must take a moment to thank Dom Damian Kearney, OSB and Dom Alban Baer, OSB. They gave me the rigor and the encouragement to hone the craft. A brief tip of the hat to the excellent faculty at the Writing Seminars at my alma mater, Johns Hopkins University. On a personal note, I am grateful for Tim Leahy, his son Mike, Tom Gallahue, Brad Roberts and Jack Trainor, whose integrity and unwavering support have buoyed me through many difficult times. Lastly, I am grateful for all who have taken the time to read my blog, especially those of you who are overseas. I thank you for your interest and the thoughtful input you have provided on the subjects. It helps me improve and do more for those I work to help. I thank my clients, not just for my daily bowl of rice, but for the opportunity to help you become the very best leaders and enterprises, purposeful and effective. It is enormously rewarding to see the good that you do for your communities. I am thankful for my business partners, who have helped me be effectively present for all of my communities. I am grateful that the light at the end of the tunnel is not another train coming in the other direction. Thanks to those relentless innovators who found ways to do things in the kind of time that the experts thought impossible. Grit ... resilience ... innovation.

About the Author

Jim Johnson's career appeared headed on a traditional business trajectory with a degree from Johns Hopkins. Instead, he veered off, spent three years in Europe, working at Alpine ski resorts and construction jobs and teaching physical education and American History in Rome. On returning to the business world, he excelled in marketing and strategy, learning from a series of good, and bad leaders. In 1990, he founded Level Three Performance Solutions. For thirty years he has thrived, developing leaders and organizations from multinationals to family held businesses. Jim lives in Reno with his wife, La Vonne. When not advising clients, he can be found officiating lacrosse games throughout Nevada and California.